For Everything

a Season

In addition to writing, Philip Gulley
also enjoys a ministry of speaking.
If you would like more information,
please contact:

David Leonards
3612 North Washington Boulevard
Indianapolis, Indiana 46205-3592
317-926-7566
intleb@prodigy.com

If you would like to correspond directly
with Philip Gulley, please send your mail to:

Philip Gulley
c/o Multnomah Publishers
Post Office Box 1720
Sisters, Oregon 97759

For Everything a Season

SIMPLE MUSINGS ON LIVING WELL

Philip Gulley

Multnomah®Publishers *Sisters, Oregon*

FOR EVERYTHING, A SEASON

published by Multnomah Publishers, Inc.
© 1999 by Philip Gulley

International Standard Book Number: 1-57673-404-8

Design by Kirk DouPonce
Cover photograph by Pat Hackett/Marco Prozzo

Printed in the United States of America
Scripture quotations are from
The Holy Bible, Revised Standard Version ©1946, 1952 by
the Division of Christian Education of the National Council of the
Churches of Christ in the United States of America.

Multnomah is a trademark of Multnomah Publishers, Inc.
and is registered in the U.S. Patent and Trademark Office.
The colophon is a trademark of Multnomah Publishers, Inc.

For information:
Multnomah Publishers, Inc.•P. O. Box 1720•Sisters, OR 97759

Library of Congress Cataloging-in-Publication Data
Gulley, Philip. For everything, a season: simple musings on living
well/Philip Gulley.   p.cm.   ISBN 1-57673-404-8 (alk. paper)
    1. Christian life–Anecdotes. 2. Gulley, Philip–Anecdotes.
    3. Christian life–Quaker authors.   I. Title
BV4517.G84   1999   98-54155
242–dc21   CIP

99 00 01 02 03 04 05 06 — 10 9 8 7 6 5 4 3 2 1

CONTENTS

Disclaimers and Dedications

For all the years I was a Quaker pastor, it was my custom at funerals to read from the third chapter of Ecclesiastes. I read it for two reasons, the first being its pure beauty. People would gasp when I concluded and would ease up to me later to ask where I had found it.

"The Bible. Old Testament. Book of Ecclesiastes," I would tell them, secretly jealous that the words were not my own.

The other reason I read it was because I found Ecclesiastes 3:1–8 to be an accurate summary of our lives, from our birth to our death and points in between. Ours is not a rose-strewn path. Alongside the time to laugh is a time to weep. I value its honesty.

In the back of my head was the idea that someone ought to write stories to these beautiful words. When no one else raised their hand to do it, I took it as a sign from the Lord that I should. This book is that effort.

It was not without struggle. Tucked alongside "a time for peace" is "a time for war." What is a Quaker pacifist to do? Whenever I come upon this phrase at the funeral reading, I declare with raised voice, "A time for peace," then drop my voice and mumble, "and a time for war." People think I'm saying "a time for more" as in "more peace," and they smile contentedly. But you can't do that in a book, so I had to face the issue head on.

I was once asked by a man if I wrote stories the way they happened or the way they should have happened. Both, I told him. While all of these stories have their origins in fact, I have been known to add a little window dressing. There was never a story anywhere that couldn't be made a little better with embellishment, so I don't apologize for that.

I dedicated my first two books, *Front Porch Tales* and *Home Town Tales*, to certain friends and family members. While I still appreciate their love and support, two dedications are enough.

This book is dedicated to a woman whose name I never caught, who approached me in a bookstore to thank me for my stories, which had been a comfort to her and her husband as he lay dying of cancer. This book is dedicated to her and to all the readers who have encouraged my ministry of writing.

I dedicate it also to my grandmother, Norma Quinett, whose tender heart even angels envied.

For Everything, a Season

ECCLESIASTES 3:1–8

For everything there is a season, and
a time for every matter under heaven:
a time to be born, and a time to die;
a time to plant, and
a time to pluck up what is planted;
a time to kill, and a time to heal;
a time to break down, and
a time to build up;
a time to weep, and a time to laugh;
a time to mourn, and a time to dance;
a time to cast away stones, and
a time to gather stones together;
a time to embrace, and
a time to refrain from embracing;
a time to seek, and a time to lose;
a time to keep, and a time to cast away;
a time to rend, and a time to sew;
a time to keep silence, and a time to speak;
a time to love, and a time to hate;
a time for war, and a time for peace.

CHAPTER ONE

A Time to Be Born

Birth Stories

I was born deep in the winter. Each birthday my father phones to recount the events surrounding my birth. Our sons are asleep in their bedroom under the eaves. My wife and I are sitting in front of the fireplace; she is doing her needlework and I am reading a mystery. The phone rings. I ease out of my chair, walk to the kitchen, pick up the phone and say, "Hello."

It is my father. No "Hello." No "How are you?" Just the same question each birthday: "Have I ever told you what happened the night you were born?"

"I don't believe so," I tell him.

"Well, it was eight o'clock in the evening

13

when your mother went into labor. I remember the time because *Gunsmoke* was just starting. There was a terrible snowstorm. We could barely see the neighbor's house for the snow. We got in the car to drive to the hospital in the city. Our defroster didn't work, and I couldn't see through the windshield. I had to drive the whole twenty miles with my head out the window. It was so cold my face was frostbitten. I ran a red light and a policeman pulled me over and said he was going to give me a ticket. I told him to hurry up because my wife was going to have a baby. The policeman said, 'Follow me!' and he turned on his lights and siren and off we went, all the way to the hospital where you were born. You had a police escort to the hospital. Not everyone can say that. That makes you special."

When I was a child, my mother would tuck me into bed, kiss my forehead, then leave the room. My father would come in and sit at the foot of my bed and ask, "Say, have I ever told you what happened the night you were born?"

"I don't believe so," I would tell him.

He would lean back, close his eyes, and conjure up that memory—the snow and the swirling red lights and the siren's wail. I've heard that story nearly forty times and I never tire of it.

Every year I wonder the same things: Will they make it in time? Will I be all right? Of course I will be, because here I am. But the way my father tells the story leaves the outcome in doubt and I never quite relax until the story concludes with me safely delivered.

In my teenage years, when my father and I were at odds, I would remember how he suffered frostbite to bring me safely into this world…and my heart would soften. I was a skinny child, the target of bullies. When beaten up and ridiculed, I would take comfort in the fact that I was ushered into this world with a police escort and they were not. It was a wonderful gift my father gave me, that story. He could not give me wealth or fame to ease my way, so he gave me that story and it provided a deep consolation.

My chief regret is that I am not able to offer my sons a similar story. Their births were routine, insofar as a child's birth is ever routine. We had sufficient time to drive to the hospital. The roads were clear. The car ran smoothly. My wife was unruffled. The doctors and nurses were competent and our children were delivered with a minimum of pain. I didn't feel a thing.

When my older son turned five years old, he asked me, "Daddy, what happened when I was born?" I didn't want to tell him the truth—that as births go, his was unremarkable, with only one peculiarity. When he was due to emerge, I was in the hospital restroom reading a back issue of *Reader's Digest*. Drama in Real Life. A man ran off the road and over a cliff, where he lay broken and dazed for three days before spelling out *HELP* with rocks and sticks. Spotted by an airplane, he was rescued and lived to share his dramatic story.

As I finished reading his harrowing tale, the nurse knocked on the door and said, "Your wife is having your baby. You better get out here." So I came out and five minutes later, so did my son. That is the truth, though it isn't the kind of story I want to tell my son. It is not the stuff of legend. So when he asked me what happened when he was born, I kissed his forehead and took my place at the foot of his bed.

"Yours was a very special birth," I told him. "Quite miraculous. It was the middle of winter. It was snowing. We were sitting in the living room late in the evening. Your mother went into labor.

We climbed into the car and made our way toward the hospital. The roads were terribly slick. As we were rounding a curve, we slid off the road and over a cliff, where our car came to rest at the bottom. We were dazed and bruised. Your mother was pinned in the wreckage and couldn't move, but I could, just barely. I managed to climb through a window and gather some sticks and rocks, which I used to spell out *HELP*. The next morning, an airplane, circling overhead, spotted us and we were rescued. We were rushed to a hospital where you were safely delivered. And that, son, is the story of your birth."

He swelled with pride. He'd had no idea his beginnings were marked with such drama. "Tell me again," he pleaded.

"Next year," I told him. "You'll have to wait until your next birthday." I kissed him good night and went downstairs to sit in my chair. My wife was there.

"What were you and Spencer talking about?" Joan asked.

"I was telling him about the night he was born," I answered.

"Did you mention how the nurse had to get you out of the restroom because you were reading that story in *Reader's Digest*?"

"Indirectly," I answered.

"I hope you haven't put ideas in his head," she said.

$\mathcal{M}$y wife is a straightforward woman who doesn't always appreciate the advantage of story and drama. She doesn't need to embellish her birth story. Her mother delivered her without assistance after the doctor had left for the day. With a birth like that, you don't need to exaggerate. It's miracle enough.

I went back upstairs to talk with Spencer. "I would prefer," I told him, "that you not talk with your mother about the car wreck and your birth. The memory of it is more than she can bear."

My birthday came a few weeks later. My parents invited us for Sunday dinner. We were seated in the dining room. I said to my father, "Tell me about my birth, about the policeman and the snow."

"What policeman?" my mother asked. "What snow?"

"The policeman who escorted you and Dad to the hospital the night I was born. Remember? It was snowing and the defroster was broken and Dad got frostbite from driving twenty miles with his head out the window."

Mom said, "It wasn't snowing—it was unusually warm that day. And he wouldn't take me to the hospital until *Gunsmoke* was over. It was his favorite show, you know. He almost named you Festus."

I looked across the table at my father. He smiled, winked, and said nothing. It was all a story—no snow, no policeman, no frostbite, no siren, no swirling lights. But it was my story, true or not, and I was grateful for it. I did not have wealth or fame or muscles or good looks to ease my way into this world. But I did have my story. My father gave it to me. It was his gift to me, bestowed with love, and I treasure it.

Later that night I was sitting in our living room. The phone rang. It was my father. "Say, have I ever told you what happened the night you were born?" he asked.

"I don't believe so," I answered.

He spoke of blowing snow and running a red light and how he got frostbite. He told about the policeman who pulled him over and the police escort with the swirling lights and the siren.

"Not everyone gets a police escort," he pointed out. "That makes you special."

These are the stories passed from father to son. We have no wealth to bestow, no fame to offer. We have only these legends to remind our children that on the day they were born, the ordinary was suspended and the miracles flew thick.

CHAPTER TWO

A Time to Die

Concerning Christian Burial

I know a lady named Alice who needs to die, and soon.

She is my friend and I don't want to her die, but die she must. And quickly. Alice and I belong to the same Quaker meeting. She has buried two husbands and has been a widow since 1957. Her husbands are buried with their first wives in their respective home towns. Her own preselected tombstone is in the Glen Cove Cemetery in Knightstown, alongside her father.

Some folks are concerned about what might happen with our computers when we hit the year 2000. That doesn't concern Alice a bit. She has a tombstone problem. Alice had her tombstone engraved in 1981 when she was seventy-six. She had her name carved on it, the year of her birth, 1905, and, believing she would die in the twentieth century, *19--* carved in for the date of death. The numbers are carved deep, so if Alice doesn't check out before the year 2000, she'll need a new tombstone.

She almost died in 1998 at the age of ninety-three, which would have solved her problem. Her son hired a woman to sit with her, but the woman took sick and Alice ended up tending her.

Alice was telling me about it. "Poor thing," she said. "She hadn't eaten well." So Alice fed her green beans, lettuce, and broccoli, and within three days both were improved. Alice attributes her own good health to clean living— no smoking, no liquor, no coffee, no soda pop, and easy on the meat. She is particularly fond of green beans, lettuce, and broccoli.

She is slowly becoming resigned to her tombstone dilemma. "It's going to be somebody else's problem," she says. "I can't worry about it." The somebody else is her son, Jack. "He'll take care of it. He's a good boy," she reports. "He'll take care of my tombstone."

Alice wants me to conduct her funeral but is concerned I'll use the occasion to slip in some liberal politics. She is, in her own words, a red-hot Republican. Her second husband was a Democrat, which he didn't reveal until after they were married. He'd voted for Eisenhower, so she assumed he was Republican. She doesn't believe in divorce so she just toughed it out. She's thinking of having the word *Republican* added to her tombstone.

I'm not certain what I want on my tombstone, or for that matter if I even want one. I am considering cremation, despite the objections of a Jehovah's Witness acquaintance who doesn't believe in cremation. He believes that when Jesus comes to establish his kingdom on earth, we'll reinhabit our bodies. Unless, of course, we've been cremated—then we're out of luck. He's found a verse in the Bible to back him up and can't be persuaded otherwise.

The reason I'd opt for cremation is because a cherry wood casket costs four thousand dollars, which is how much I earned the first year I worked. Though I make more than four thousand dollars a year now, that figure is embedded in my mind as a year's wage. I worked at Johnston's IGA sacking groceries, stacking empty pop bottles, mopping up busted pickle jars, and sweeping the parking lot. I worked every day after school and all day Saturday and earned four thousand dollars. I'm not about to spend that money on a casket, even one made of cherry wood.

The Oldenburg Casket Company is headquartered in Indiana. They are one of the world's largest manufacturers of caskets—700,000 units a year. The increasing popularity of cremation knocks that number down a bit each year. Their cheapest casket retails for 225 dollars and is made of particle board. If you're a ward of the state, that's what you'll get when you die.

Their most expensive casket sells for twenty thousand dollars. It's pure bronze with twenty-four karat gold hardware, lined with velvet and with rounded corners. This is the casket for queens and presidents. It is guaranteed for seventy-five years, so if you dig up your loved one seventy-four years down the road and the casket is damaged, they'll replace it for free. If the Oldenburg Casket Company goes out of business before then, you're out of luck. The particle board casket is guaranteed for thirty days.

I know an Amish man who makes pine-box caskets with rope handles for one hundred dollars. That's a fair price for a casket. I'm thinking of buying one and storing it in my garage so it'll be there when I need it. He guarantees his pine-box caskets for one hundred years. He says if you come back in a hundred years needing the casket replaced, he'll build you a new one for free.

If I were buried in a casket, I'd have to be interred in a graveyard, which I don't want. The place I want to be buried is in the field behind my parents' barn, under the pine tree where we buried our dog Zipper in 1977. Since our town prohibits backyard burials, cremation is looking more attractive. I want my ashes next to Zipper, either spread on the ground or buried in a canister. It makes no difference to me. If my wife desires, she can have her ashes put there also. She didn't know Zipper but I think they'd have gotten along just fine.

Concerning music, there are certain songs I'd like at my funeral, namely "Blessed Assurance," "Abide with Me," and "Leaning on the Everlasting Arms." I would also like Mozart played, but only if it can be done well. If not, skip it. I don't want any rock music. This is a trend I'm seeing when younger people die and I'm not for it. If it wasn't written before 1940, I don't want it sung or played at my funeral.

I hope careful thought is given to who preaches my funeral. I don't want somebody giving an altar call. People feel guilty enough at funerals without having more guilt heaped on. I would prefer a bighearted preacher giving my eulogy, someone inclined to widen heaven's doors. I don't want to leave folks wondering whether I made it.

As a Quaker pastor, I've presided over numerous funerals. Except we don't call them funerals, we call them memorial services. We sit around and say nice things about the deceased, whether they deserve it or not. Then we read the Twenty-third Psalm and quote from the Gospel of John about heavenly mansions. Chock-full of Quakers, we speculate. Simple Quakers in simple mansions.

Alice believes all her family are there—her mother and father, her eight brothers and sisters, her two husbands. She loved both her husbands and isn't sure with which one she'll share a mansion. I'm betting on the Republican.

It used to be cheap to die, but not anymore. There are casket makers, cemetery owners, florists, musicians, morticians, tombstone carvers, embalming fluid salesmen, and gravediggers. Everyone has a hand out. Dying has become big business in America, tens of billions of dollars a year. That's just a guess; the Oldenburg Casket Company wouldn't confirm it. When it comes to money, they're tight-lipped, which makes me think there's lots of money in it.

If I were dying, the last person I'd spend time with is the mortician. First, I'd play pitch-and-catch with my sons. They're always asking me to throw the ball with them and too often I'm telling them I don't have the time. It's a cruel thing to tell your children you don't have time for them. I hope they don't remember that about me.

Then I'd call my father and ask him to tell me the story of my birth one last time, how I was brought into this world against stunning odds. It fills me with confidence, knowing that God has been pulling for me since birth.

With those commitments met, I would hasten to my wife. I'd ask her forgiveness for the many times I cared more for my happiness than hers. For the first eight years of our marriage

Joan worked full time to put me through college. I repaid her by being a grouch and not helping with the housework. The day we married, we each vowed to serve the other. My wife has taken that pledge far more seriously than I.

That done, I would speak to the good Lord about his heavenly mansions to see if there were vacancies. I wouldn't be picky. I'd sooner have a broom closet in the house of the Lord than a mansion down below. Finally, I'd open my Gentle Shepherd Hymnal to number 452, "Leaning on the Everlasting Arms," and I would sing to the heavens. I'd sing of blessed peace with my Lord so near, then snuggle deep in my pine-box casket, safe and secure from all alarms.

Death jogs our minds about what's most important. It separates wheat from chaff. Life isn't about money and big houses or fancy cars and titles. It's about family and friends and our relationship with God and whether we love. We can't fit all that on a tombstone, so we carve our names and our dates of birth and death and hope that, somewhere between those two dates, life was well lived.

CHAPTER THREE

A Time to Plant

Marvin

*I have never had so many good ideas,
day after day, as when I worked in a garden.*
JOHN ERSKINE

If what John Erskine says is true, it explains why for the past ten years I've suffered a drought of good ideas. It's been that long since we've planted a garden.

Now we're back to gardening, even though our neighborhood covenant forbids gardens that are visible from the street. I live on a corner, so anything I do in my yard is visible from the street. The covenant makes no allowance for my predicament. It is straightforward: *No garden shall be visible from any street.* Though the zoning zealots aren't specific, they are obviously referring to vegetable gardens because flower gardens abound in the front yards of our neighborhood. It's vegetables they don't like.

I don't know who made this rule; someone not from around here. This is Indiana, after all, the Crown Jewel of the Great Midwest, the Bread Basket of America. Most of us are only a generation or two away from the farm and prefer our vegetables fresh from the garden, not from Argentina. We swore on our parents' graves never to eat vegetables wrapped in plastic with freshness dates. We want to brush the dirt off our vegetables ourselves. It is a matter of integrity.

There is rebellion in our neighborhood. People are breaking the garden rule right and left. Most violate the rule discreetly. They hide tomato plants behind lilac bushes and tuck their green beans amongst their marigolds. Others of us sin more openly, with boldness. We call up Dave Kisner, who comes with his tractor in broad daylight, drops the plow, and leaves deep furrows in his wake, visible two streets away. We do not confine ourselves to shy, demure vegetables like beets and onions. We plant pole beans and towering corn and hulking pumpkins and melons. We are proud of our vegetables and we flaunt them.

Our garden measures twenty-five feet wide by thirty feet long, small by Indiana standards. We have three rows of cutting flowers—zinnias, sweet williams, cosmos, dinner-plate dahlias, and grey-striped sunflowers. In the vegetable department, we grow broccoli, Early Girl tomatoes, purple teepee beans, green beans, pumpkins, and sweet corn. We ring the garden with marigolds to keep the rabbits out.

As gardens go, ours is a good one, which serves two purposes nicely: providing food for our table and teaching our sons the value of honest labor. It is their garden. They hoe the weeds and carry the water. They do not uproot every weed and their watering is indiscriminate; some plants are drowned while others groan with thirst, but my sons are growing muscles and a respect for nature and hard work.

The problem with America is that we don't garden as much as we once did. There are no rules against video games and television in our neighborhood, which is how many children pass their time. I would outlaw those character-numbing blights and require gardens. Gardens grow more than vegetables; they grow character. I don't know this for a fact, but I bet these schoolkids who go berserk and shoot their classmates have never worked in a garden. If they had, they'd appreciate the fragility of life and, having labored to bring it along, would be less inclined to snuff it out.

Some of the finest people I know keep gardens. Marvin Rutledge lives on Broadway Street, around the corner from my parents. He moved there in 1943 with Lorena, his bride. Their first spring they put in a garden and they've been at it ever since. Marvin's garden is 300 feet long and 120 feet wide, not quite a football field but close. When they first planted their garden, they planted half of it in sorghum. Four months later, they'd harvest the sorghum and sell it to the mill south of town. Marvin and Lorena had three little girls and the sorghum crop financed their school shoes. Now the girls are grown and gone, along with the mill, so Marvin doesn't plant sorghum anymore.

Marvin is a big believer in sorghum. He keeps a Tupperware bottle of it on his kitchen table and eats sorghum every morning for breakfast. He says it keeps you regular. He also likes okra and tends two long rows of it in his garden. That's a lot of okra. He loves rhubarb. The west edge of his garden is planted in rhubarb, three hundred feet worth. The secret to growing good rhubarb, Marvin says, is to put a lump or two of water-softener salt in the hole before you plant the rhubarb. The salt in the green bag that you get at Krogers. Marvin swears by it.

Marvin has two rows of tomatoes. Lorena cans them, then puts them down in their cellar on the shelves. Some people have wine cellars; in Indiana we have tomato cellars. Marvin advises pinching off the top blossom of the tomato plant if you want a lot of tomatoes. If you don't want a lot of tomatoes, then leave that top blossom alone.

Every winter, Marvin and Lorena drive to Florida where they have a trailer. They carry their clothes in the backseat and their okra, rhubarb, and tomatoes in the trunk. The sorghum sits between them on the front seat. Marvin drives and Lorena rides shotgun. When Marvin gets hungry, Lorena fixes him a peanut butter and sorghum sandwich and down the road they go. They are like that in all their efforts—a harmonious team.

Some people, old-timers mostly, garden by the signs. They plant certain crops during certain phases of the moon. It's common to pass by a garden at midnight and see someone mounding potatoes, their lantern aglow. I know farmers who never do anything on their farm except by the signs. They wait until the sign of Capricorn to slaughter their pigs so the meat won't shrink. Dig post holes smack in between the full and new moons so the poles won't wobble. They have their dental work done in February, under the sign of Aquarius, and paint their house when the signs point to Aries or Leo. I asked Marvin if he planted by the signs. He said he never followed the signs, that the best time to do something was when you had the time.

I can't take credit for our garden. We inherited it from the people who lived here before us. There is a farm market on the square every Saturday; we'd have been content to buy our vegetables there. But since the ground was already turned up, we put in half a dozen tomato plants. Then Marvin encouraged us to plant some pole beans, which led to broccoli, which led to sweet corn. We drew the line at okra.

According to Genesis 2:8, the first garden ever was planted by God. "And the Lord God planted a garden in Eden, in the east; and there he put the man whom he had formed." Unfortunately, it didn't work out. The man wasn't much help, plus God put trees in the garden, which is ill advised. Trees mean shade and gardens need full sun. That could have been some of the problem.

The last time I went to visit Marvin, half his garden was plowed but not planted. I asked him what he was going to grow there. "Grass," he told me and hung his head a little. "Garden's getting bigger and I'm getting older." He's talking about selling his place and wants to know if I'm interested. Marvin's house is one hundred years old and his garden almost sixty. I didn't think I have the wherewithal to keep either one going and I told him so.

We sat in his kitchen and ate peanut butter and sorghum sandwiches. Marvin told me he's hoping to sell to a gardener. He hopes the new owner will allow him to come back and sit underneath the maple tree behind the garage, where he's sat for sixty years, listening to his vegetables. "You can hear the corn grow," he says. "In July, after a rain, if you sit real still, you can hear the corn grow."

Sometimes in deep summer when I'm eating

sweet corn, I think of buying Marvin's house and planting his garden in corn. I'd set out two chairs underneath the maple tree—one for Marvin and one for me. On July evenings, after a rain, we'd sit together and listen to the corn grow and all would be well. I think when God made his garden, that is maybe what he had in mind.

Once read an article which speculated on the location of the Garden of Eden. Somewhere in the Middle East, the author believed. He's way off. I know where that garden is and I know the man who's been tending it. I've shaken his hand and eaten his sorghum.

CHAPTER FOUR

A Time to Pluck Up What Is Planted

The Harvest

Officially, summer ends around September 21. The *Farmer's Almanac* states the very minute when summer ends and fall begins. It has to do with the position of the sun and earth. But the almanac doesn't take into account other, more telling, factors. For me, summer ends when the sunflower stalks in our garden crumple over, the tomato vines wither, and the pumpkins deepen to orange. Some years that happens weeks before the twenty-first day of September, some years weeks after. You don't need the *Farmer's Almanac* to tell when summer is past.

There is a wonderful harmony to harvest and autumn. The sweet corn dies just as the neighbors tire of our leaving it on their doorstep. Sweet corn has the good sense to know when enough is enough. Zucchini is just the opposite. It is a profoundly stupid vegetable, always wearing out its welcome. One year we planted a row of zucchini and were reduced to leaving sacks of it in the unlocked cars at church. That never happens with sweet corn.

In our home, plucking up what we've planted is a treasured time. We can scarcely wait for the first green beans to ripen. My boys sit on the porch swing, the beans between them, and snap them into the kettle at their feet. Joan fries bacon, boils the beans quick, drains the water to get the green taste out, starts over with fresh water, then stirs in the bacon. If green beans had been served at the Last Supper, Judas would never have gotten up to leave, I promise you that.

My father enjoys everything about gardening except the harvest. He likes the smell of plow-turned earth. Stretching out a string to mark the rows is pure delight. He is eager to plant, hoe, and water. These are burdens the rest of us endure in order to savor the harvest. But at harvesttime, my father is a complete flop. He is tired of gardens and wants nothing more to do with them.

Tomatoes rot, beans shrivel, corn toughens. A vegetable holocaust.

He tends a small corner of Marvin Rutledge's garden. When I see Marvin at Quaker meeting, he tells me, "Remind your father to come pick his vegetables." But I can't budge him. People come to visit Marvin, to marvel at his long, abundant rows. Marvin points to my father's corner, to the dying produce. "That's not my corner," he says. "That belongs to Norm Gulley." Marvin spent sixty years building a reputation as a master gardener, but is fast becoming tainted by my father's inaction.

Unlike my dad, I relish the harvest—the buckets of tomatoes, the baskets of beans, and especially the pumpkins. Our first summer of gardening, we planted ten mounds of pumpkins. By July they were sprawled throughout the garden, lounging amongst the tomatoes and the beans. Other gardeners stopped by to witness their spread and chuckle, pointing out that it's customary to give pumpkins an entire patch rather than crowding them between the sunflowers and the beans.

"It's my wife's garden," I pointed out. "She

planted it, along with my boys. I was gone when they did it. Out of state."

Joan shooed them away. "Just wait until fall. They'll be begging for a pumpkin," she told me.

First the sweet corn petered out. Then the beans and the tomatoes. We dried the sunflowers and stored the seeds for the redbirds. The marigolds sputtered to an end. We mercy-killed the zucchini. Then came the pumpkins, elbowing their way across the garden and invading the yard. At first, while mowing the yard, I carefully steered around them. Then, alarmed with their aggressiveness, I set a boundary. No going past the clothesline. Any pumpkin crossing it would be hacked to pieces by my Snapper.

The next few weeks my mowing was punctuated by the loud reports of massacred pumpkins. Pumpkin innards were splattered across our yard. My boys watched, terrified, peeking between their fingers. Years from now they will awaken, trembling and screaming, dreaming of pumpkins shooting out the sides of mowers.

By October, twenty pumpkins had survived. I granted them amnesty. The autumn leaves were at their peak, startling in their beauty. The nights were chilly. Bedroom windows, open since April, were closed shut. I waxed my lawn mower, drained the gas, and pushed it to the corner of the garage. I unhooked the garden hose from the spigot, coiled it up, and hung it on a nail in the basement. Autumn preparations.

On a Saturday afternoon we got in the truck and drove to my parents' house with our twenty pumpkins. My sister was there with her three boys. My brother came out from the city. There was a scattering of neighborhood kids. Dad was building the bonfire. Mom was sitting off to the side, straightening wire hangers to roast hot dogs and marshmallows. My entire family is a little different, not quite normal. I suspect it is due to the lead paint from the wire hangers we've used to roast our wieners.

*D*espite its somber air, I savor fall's restful beauty. It provides a colorful calm in our otherwise busy lives, a time for wiener roasts, pumpkin carving, and trips to Beasley's Orchard.

Beasley's Orchard sits east of town on old Highway 36. New Highway 36 is a mile south— loud, fast, and pushy. It is a Type-A road. Old Highway 36 is tranquil. Farmhouses sit back

from the road, rooted in time. It is the road for
minstrels and poets, for people who treasure the
journey over the destination. Beasley's Orchard
sits amongst the farmhouses. Row after row of
winesaps, Granny Smiths, and Early Blaze spill
down to the roadside. Were you to pause and
remember, I'm sure you could recall such an
orchard yourself.

Joyce Lakin bakes apple cobbler at the
orchard every fall. People drive out from the city
on Saturday afternoons, walking the rows, wishing they could live among such quiet splendor.
The rows steer them toward the barn, where
Joyce serves the cobbler.

"Do you make this cobbler here?" they ask.
They always ask that. Joyce smiles and assures
them, "Yes, we do."

They buy a serving of cobbler. Then they
buy a gallon of cider, caramel apples, and a stick
of horehound candy. Later in the season, when
the pumpkins come on, Joyce adds pumpkin
pie to the list. I thought of taking my pumpkins
to her but decided instead to take them to the
family wiener roast. We unloaded the pumpkins
from the truck and spread them on the ground.
The children wandered among them, weighing
the merits of each one and making their selec-

tions. They hauled their pumpkins to the picnic table where my father cut fist-sized holes in their tops. The children reached down inside and felt the slippery innards. They grimaced but plunged ahead.

The older children carve their own pumpkins. The younger children draw faces on the pumpkins and the menfolk carve them. Carving their own pumpkin will become a rite of passage. I can tell. I know my sons. Every October they will ask, "Is this the year?" I have decided that the year they carve their first pumpkin will be the Christmas they receive their first pocket-knife. It will be a sweet year for them. When the knife plunges into the pumpkin and the wet pumpkin smell rises up and takes me back, that is the sure sign that summer is spent.

I lay down my knife and pause, then thank the Lord for another year of bounty, for healthy boys and a tender wife, and friends who snicker at my pumpkins in summer and yearn for them in fall.

CHAPTER FIVE

A Time to Kill

A Careful Subtraction

here are certain things every town has at
least one of, no matter the town's size. There
is always a sneaky politician who makes sure the
road in front of his house gets paved first. There
is always a water tower. And there is always a
family who owned the grain mill years ago and
lives in the nicest house in town, generally on a
hill.

Since this is a small town and I have to live
here, I'll be the first to declare that all the politicians in our town are true statesmen, free of
corruption and wise beyond their years. We
have two water towers. The old water tower was
built in 1892 and sits behind Harry Christie's

house. The new water tower, erected in 1960, is located next to the elementary school. The nicest house in town is owned by the Blantons, who ran the grain mill. Their home crowns a hill north of town. Though I've lived here a good many years, first through my childhood and now after recently moving back, I never tire of walking past the Blanton house and admiring it as it nestles amongst the trees.

The Blantons built the house during the Great Depression. They bought the land from a man named Carter, who was mean to his wife and an embarrassment to the town. We were glad to see him leave, and because the Blantons expedited his departure we've had a high opinion of them ever since. Mr. Blanton is deceased. Mrs. Blanton still lives in the house on the hill, soldiering on. When she turned ninety-three, her daughter hired a nurse to stay with her. To pass the time, Mrs. Blanton and her nurse work outside, tending the acreage and pulling weeds.

The original Blanton estate is just shy of eighty acres, most of it rolling woods and meadows. In our growing-up years, Bill Eddy and I spent countless nights camping in those woods. We slapped mosquitoes in July and burrowed deep in our sleeping bags in January. We never asked permission to camp there and took a strong delight in trespassing, excited at the prospect of getting away with something. I feel a similar thrill whenever I drive through a yellow light.

The woods are a place of firsts for me. I smoked my first, and only, cigar in those woods. Kissed my first girl alongside its creek on a Saturday afternoon in autumn, and, six months later, when the girl no longer welcomed my kisses, was healed of heartbreak while hiking its trails. I learned to shoot a .22 rifle there. And in those woods I discovered the quiet peace of a campfire on a snapping autumn evening.

I am now walking those same trails with my two little boys—Spencer on my right, Sam on my left. They hold my pant legs with one hand and grasp their toy rifles with the other, cocked and ready for grizzly bears. I make a growling sound and their eyes open wide, their rifles swing up, and their hands quiver with such excitement I can feel it through my pant legs.

When our sons were two and five, a house beside the woods came on the market. I was driving by and saw the For Sale sign, drove to the realtor's office, paid fifty dollars earnest money, then drove back to the city to tell my wife, who understood perfectly the lure of first kisses, healed hearts, and lurking grizzlies. Five months later, a moving van carried our earthly belongings across two counties and here we are, just down the road from Mrs. Blanton and her nurse.

I've not been the only one attracted to Mrs. Blanton's woods. Developers have been after her to sell it. They want to knock down the trees, scrape the earth raw, pipe up the creeks, pack the land with houses, and name it Wooded Glen or some other hint of what it was before the carnage. They spoke to her of big money, which wasn't her language. Then, to their eternal dismay, she donated the land to the town for a nature preserve, with the understanding that it remain forever off limits to real estate predators. Little boys toting toy rifles are quite welcome.

The town hired a woman to manage the preserve. Her name is Kim. Her college degree is in geology. She is not a naturalist and made that clear right up front. "I know rocks and geologic formations. I'm learning about plants, but there's still a lot I don't know. I'm not a naturalist," she told the park director, who hired her anyway.

The Blanton Woods Nature Preserve opens every morning at precisely eight o'clock and closes around 5 P.M., give or take an hour. Kim unlocks the gate every morning and since my boys and I live next to the preserve, we close the gate at five o'clock. Kim is punctual. We are not. Sometimes the preserve stays open way past supper, when we finally remember to close the gate. One morning I awoke and remembered that we hadn't closed the gate the night before. I had to sneak over and close it before Kim arrived to open it.

Our town encompasses exactly 5.7 square miles. I suspect the preserve is the only section that remains relatively unchanged in the past seventy years. The deep ravines and the four creeks coursing through the preserve discourage settlement. It is not an easy woods to tame. Still, there is a movement afoot to restore the meadows to their 1824 state, when our ancestors first built along the big creek. When they arrived in May of 1824, the meadows along the creek waved with prairie grass and wildflowers—little bluestem, butterfly weed, switchgrass, prairie cinquefoil, and wild rye. Now those native beauties are choked out by ironweed, black medic, pokeweed, horse nettle, and joe-pye weed. Squatters all. The plan is to kill off the interlopers and replant the meadow in native grasses and wildflowers. Kim is in charge of taking it back to the way it was, though killing off the plants, even joe-pye weeds, is repugnant to her. Still, for the sake of the schoolchildren who tour this place every spring, she is proceeding.

She told me, "I want the kids to see how Indiana was before the strip malls and interstates."

Though I understand her reluctance, I am for the killing, for dispensing with these interlopers and letting butterfly weed and prairie cinquefoil have a fresh go at it. I figure it is the least we owe nature, to even the score. We have our 5.7 square miles. I see nothing wrong with letting nature have her eighty acres. Besides, with butterfly weed, prairie cinquefoil, and switchgrass come bluebirds, a handsome dividend. But there is another principle at work here, the Principle of Giving Way. Our 1824 ancestors knew this principle. They observed that death must happen for life to follow. The plant is born, but first the seed must die. Joe-pye weed has had its day. Now is the time for prairie cinquefoil.

We are not much different from these meadows. If certain things take root in us, it will be to our demise. I consider how certain of my faults cripple my nobler qualities and thus require killing—my lusts that choke out love, my self-concern that crowds out empathy. My reluctance to put these faults to death serves only to enslave me.

Patrick Morley writes of the "half-surrendered life": This is when we add God to our lives without subtracting those things which choke out God's joyous, holy presence—our twisted priorities, our greed, our slavish devotion to comfort. It is not enough to subtract some of these encumbrances. They all must go.

When Mrs. Blanton and her nurse tend the flower beds, they do not uproot some weeds while allowing others to flourish. With some things we ought make no peace. On my way to lock the gate, I walk past and see them stooping and pulling. It is a methodical killing. So too does life in God's reign require the careful subtraction of all which keeps joy at bay.

CHAPTER SIX

A Time to Heal

One September

The day Adam Brooks died was as fine an autumn day as there is in Indiana. School was in full swing, the high school Homecoming was that weekend, and the first book fair of the year was underway at South Elementary School.

My wife was at the book fair, sorting through the books, when she heard a siren off in the distance. When Joan determined that it wasn't headed for our house and for her children, she returned to her sorting. Then mothers came in talking about a bad wreck on the highway, and within a few hours the word was out that some teenagers had crashed on the highway west of town. One of the boys, Adam Brooks, was dead.

In this town of five thousand people, in three years' time, five of our high schoolers have perished in car wrecks. Angela Cook, Elisha Holt, Jacqueline Quandt, Derek Ellis, and now, Adam Brooks. They were all fine children, and when I consider the sad carnage I find myself wishing the automobile had never been invented.

I did not know these children well, though I had met Jacqueline Quandt, who lived down the street from my parents. I saw her every Labor Day at the neighborhood party. She was an attractive, vivacious young lady with big plans. I learned of her death from my mother who, on hearing of Jacqueline's death, immediately phoned her own children to confirm their well-being. A mother's first instinct. Neighbors gathered at the Quandt home to console the parents. Father Vince came from Saint Mary's. The men stood with Jacqueline's father while mothers clutched around Jacqueline's mother. It rips your heart out to consider the many times this scene has been replayed in our small town.

We are becoming experts at grieving. The local ministers head to the high school, where they counsel and comfort the students.

The fire department visits the elementary school, where they teach the children to always buckle up. The undertakers rearrange the funeral parlor furniture to accommodate the flood of mourners. The police department plans the funeral procession. The politicians talk of raising the driving age. The parents ache and for the next few evenings, sneak into their children's bedrooms and gaze upon them sleeping, grateful for their good health.

The day Adam Brooks died, the high school students told their teachers they weren't in the mood to finish their floats and march in a Homecoming parade. Homecoming was postponed. On the day Adam was buried, I was driving my son to kindergarten when the funeral procession, which began at the high school, drove past. I counted 120 cars; Weaver's Funeral Home didn't have enough funeral flags for all the cars in Adam's procession. The students were dressed in their church clothes, their faces somber and tear-streaked. They wound their way down Mackey Road to Lincoln Street to the South Cemetery. A long, sad line. I looked over at my son sitting beside me in the car and vowed to myself that he would not drive until he turned eighteen. If the politicians won't make it the law, I will.

The week after Adam died, we were building a new playground at the town park. We had saved our money for a year, $80,000 worth, and in five days' time we built a playground for our children. Seven hundred people volunteered their help. Two shifts a day for five days. Thousands of meals cooked and served. Like an Amish barn-raising. I went twice to watch but couldn't bring myself to help. I am not a handy person and didn't want to drag the project down. I wandered among the workers, listening to snatches of conversation about Adam. Sad voices and resigned sighs.

There is a healing power to labor. I don't know if sorrow can be sweated away, but the pain seems to soften. The building starts with a somber silence and by week's end there is laughter. The high school shop class comes to help. The students sand the wood and bolt the race cars together. Smaller children bring their paints and paint murals on the castle walls. On Sunday afternoon, the last rough edge is sanded, the ribbon is cut, and swarms of children scramble over the playground. It is a balm to the soul of this wonderful town.

*H*omecoming was held the next Friday. The floats lined up at the old school along with the marching band, the fire department, the Homecoming princesses, the exchange students, and the Junior League football teams. Exum Hadley, unaware of the parade's path, turned his pickup truck onto Washington Street and found himself in the parade, smack in between the freshman float and the exchange student from Moldavia. A block later he turned smartly to the left and broke free. "I'm glad my truck was nice and clean," he told me later.

Our family sat on the curb in front of the Stevenson-Jensen Insurance Agency watching the parade. As each unit passed, they threw candy to the children. The marching band stepped by, then a group of high schoolers carrying a white banner. *Adam—In Our Hearts Forever,* it read. Then the freshman float rolled past and the exchange student from Moldavia, looking slightly bewildered. The parade coursed through town out to the high school, where that night our football team beat Greencastle by a fearsome number of points. Most of the town was there, crowding the sidelines and cheering. At halftime, Amanda Smale was crowned

Homecoming Queen. Smiles amongst the tears.

The next morning, Saturday, saw the return of Swap and Shop Days to the town square. Years ago it had been an annual event, but when our town square grew ugly with empty buildings, we disbanded it. Now, five years later, new trees grow along the sidewalks. Stores are returning to life. Old-fashioned lampposts line streets paved with brick. A new fountain splashes a song of serenity. Benches have returned to the courthouse lawn along with the old men who sit on them.

Dennis Dawes sang the national anthem and the marching band played "Back Home Again in Indiana." Jeff Martin gave a fine speech about our town's origins and yet another ribbon was cut. Ribbon cuttings two weekends in a row—a record for our town. People wandered from booth to booth and in and out of stores, sipping cider and buying wooden shelves with heart-shaped cutouts.

My wife and I took our sons to the historical museum, housed in the old jail, and showed them the jail cells, dropping dark hints about the importance of obeying their parents and not fighting with each other. Then we went to the Friends meeting-house where the ladies of the meeting were serving chicken and noodles and raffling off a quilt. Money for missions, for people in faraway countries who haven't been blessed as we have.

*I*t is easy, on sweet days like that, to forget that just down the road a mother and father grieve. In those homes, grief isn't healed with labor or parades or football or Swap and Shop Days. You walk past and see the shades drawn and you remember, with a sharp intake of breath, the sorrow that befell those families. You feel guilty that, five minutes earlier, you were happy and laughing when such deep pain was only a stone's throw away. Your mind turns to Angela, Elisha, Jacqueline, Derek, and now Adam, and you draw your children close.

"Stay out of the street," you warn them. "Come up here next to Daddy, on the sidewalk."

So begins a slow healing, which for those of us on the sidewalks is a far quicker process. Soon entire days will pass without a thought of the deceased. Then we will see a mother at the store, still hollow-eyed with grief, and it will come back to us and we will despise ourselves for forgetting. But on quiet Sunday mornings we remember and pray for their healing, and we draw our children close and speak soft and tender words.

CHAPTER SEVEN

A Time to Break Down

These Fleeting Years

When my grandparents turned eighty, our family began speculating about who would be the first to go. Grandpa, we decided, because he'd smoked a pipe for fifty years and would die of cancer. Thus we were surprised when, at the age of eighty-eight, Grandma fell off their back porch, broke her hip, and died after complications. She fell one week and the next week we were at Gardner's Funeral Home receiving consolations.

Four years later, we still can't believe she's gone and catch ourselves looking forward to Sunday dinners and Grandma's strawberry dessert. After Grandma died, we thought

Grandpa would soon follow. But he had a dog to care for, and the responsibility revived him. This follows a pattern. My grandfather has always been underestimated and has spent his life doing things people thought quite unlikely.

At the age of ninety-two, Grandpa and his dog went to live in a retirement home. Before he moved, he called me over to his house to give me his woodworking tools. He stayed at the retirement home for three days, then returned to his house on Hickory Drive. He called to tell me he had moved back. I told him I was happy for him, but if he thought I was going to return his tools, he was crazy.

I asked him why he moved back.

There was no place for Babe to run, he told me. Babe is his dog. He is squat and round. The fur on his belly is worn off from dragging the ground. He hasn't run in five years, but Grandpa still imagines him to be fleet and frisky, a perpetual puppy. Grandpa opens the back door and Babe drags himself out to the yard, where he collapses in a heap. After a while, he struggles to his feet, does what he came outside to do, then drags himself back in. You time this dog with a calendar, not a stopwatch.

Grandpa moves at a similar pace. It is sad to see. When I was a child and we would walk the four blocks into town, I ran to keep even with him. Now I pick him up for Sunday dinner and it takes five minutes to negotiate the thirty feet from front door to car door. This is the same man who, on his sixty-eighth birthday, pedaled a bicycle one hundred miles. He hasn't made his peace with legs that won't do as he commands. It bothers him, I can tell. He drops into the car seat and shakes his head in frustration.

"This is horrible," he declares. "I hate being old."

His driving days ended after a series of scrapes and bumps, culminating in a near-miss with a gas pump at Larry Waterman's gas station. The idea of Grandpa leaving this world in a ball of fire was more than we could bear, so we persuaded him to surrender his license.

He had taken a driver's exam to renew his license. He told me how the driving examiner had cowered in the passenger seat, yelling, "Those are mailboxes! Those are mailboxes!"

"Like I don't know a mailbox when I hit one," Grandpa said.

Without a license, Grandpa was stuck at home and began casting about for alternative transportation. He needed a way to get to the Sunshine Cafe, the Pizza Hut, and the Seniors Center. He read a newspaper circular advertising a Sears riding mower. He thought of buying one, removing the mower deck, and riding the tractor back and forth to town.

"What kind of mileage do you suppose they get?" he asked me.

I called Sears and asked the man in the tractor department. He wasn't sure. He told me the cutting width—thirty-eight inches. I told him we were interested in mileage, not cutting width. I don't think he'd ever been asked that before. I put a gallon of gas in my tractor, put it in third gear, and rode north out of town past Ron Randolph's house. Turned east on 500 North and went two miles to Maplewood Road. Then aimed back south and went one mile before running out of gas in front of Ernie Helton's place. Ernie gave me a gallon of gas to get home. When I got home I called Grandpa on the phone and told him a tractor gets eight miles to the gallon in third gear.

"That's not very good mileage," he said. "I wonder how much a golf cart costs."

Three thousand, two hundred, seventy-five dollars and forty-eight cents, I discovered. Plus tax. And it's against the law to ride them on the street, though the policeman in our town said he'd look the other way as long as Grandpa stuck to the side roads. "I can't have him riding up and down Main Street in a golf cart," he told us.

Grandpa finally settled on a three-wheeled electric scooter. A man from the city came out to give him a demonstration. Grandpa kicked the tires and drove the scooter around the block. "I'll take it," he told the man, and wrote out a check.

Grandpa's electric scooter has two speeds—turtle and rabbit. He lets me ride it, but only if I promise not to shift it up to rabbit. He rides his scooter to the Seniors Center for lunch. If he has a good reason, he'll ride it to the Sunshine Cafe or Pizza Hut for supper. Grandpa is of the generation that needs to justify eating out. Eating out because you want to is not reason enough. But with his newfound mobility, Grandpa now uses the slimmest of occasions to justify eating supper at Pizza Hut or Sunshine Cafe. National Teachers Day, Epiphany, Flag Day, Arbor Day,

Canada Day, and the day we switch to Daylight
Savings Time are all fine days to celebrate with a
meal out, Grandpa contends. And a host of
other holidays, foreign and domestic.

My grandfather is a marvel to me. He
worked close to forty years as a glass
cutter before the company folded and he lost his
pension. When most men are retiring, he took
college classes and went to work for an architec-
tural firm. He worked well into his eighties. If it
is possible to live on sheer determination, my
grandfather will last into his hundreds.

But it is not possible, and we are witnessing
a slow surrender, a breaking down. The paint on
his front door is chipped and needs scraping.
His back porch now gets swept once a week
instead of once a day. Those things tend to be
overlooked as we struggle to keep his lawn
mowed, his clothes washed, and his carpet vac-
uumed. Rather than complaining about what
isn't getting done, he is grateful for our help.
This is also a change—his obvious gratitude. It
makes helping him less a duty and more a joy.

One day, after mowing his lawn, I went
inside to visit with him. We talked of death, his

and mine, and how we wanted to pass. He declared he was ready, that he wanted to be with Grandma. I told him I was not yet ready to die, but that I knew how I wanted to go.

"How is that?" he asked.

"I want to be shot by a jealous husband while climbing through a bedroom window at the age of ninety," I told him.

Grandpa didn't laugh. What I intend as a joke, he takes literally. Now he is worried that I will become a philanderer and disgrace the family name, yet another burden to carry in his old age.

There are times when I don't see him for several weeks. When I see him I am surprised at his decline. Were I to see him every day, I would not likely notice this slow breaking down. So when I do see him, I am invariably alarmed and slightly panicked. Grandpa is fading, I think to myself. One day we'll come here and let ourselves in and he'll be lying in bed, drawn up and still.

He senses it too, that the time to give his account is drawing near. In these last years, his interests have turned heavenward. When the Baptist minister visits the Seniors Center, Grandpa listens a little closer. He asks me questions about heaven and whether he'll make it. Grandma is there, he is certain, and the prospect of not being with her is more than he can bear. I assure him they will be together.

On the fourth anniversary of Grandma's passing, I ate lunch with Grandpa at the Seniors Center. He said to me, "Grandma died four years ago today." Then he pushed his plate back and said he didn't feel like eating.

I wonder why he lingers, why this slow breaking down. Maybe to learn something. I'm not certain. I know I'm learning. I'm learning the mileage of a garden tractor, how much a golf cart costs, and, most importantly, to appreciate my wife in these oh-so-fleeting years.

CHAPTER EIGHT

A Time to Build

Concerning Screen Doors and Shaker Chairs

The best thing about my mother-in-law Ruby's farmhouse is her old-fashioned screen door. It is made of wood, has a spring attached, locks with a hook-and-eye latch, and closes with a loud *whap*.

I like to sit on her back porch and listen to the door whap. Ruby knows when she has a good thing. A neighbor once suggested she put a rubber stop on the door so it wouldn't whap, and Ruby glared at him.

For years we lived in rented homes, then bought our own home when we moved back here. The man who inspected it made out a list of things we needed to tend to—electrical matters, termites, and other minor concerns. "Those can wait," I told my wife. "What this house needs is an old-fashioned screen door."

A month later I ran into Terry Bolton while I was at the hardware store buying paint for my porch swing. Terry is the man in our town you call when you need something built. I'd been away from home nearly twenty years. The last time I saw Terry he was an eighth-grader delivering newspapers. Now he is an artisan, a craftsman of the old school, who is to wood what Rembrandt was to paint. My parents live in a century-old house. The windows are curved, built with the kind of wood you can't find anymore. When the windows needed replacing, carpenter after carpenter recommended tearing them out and starting from scratch with vinyl windows, which to my parents was a desecration, akin to spitting on a grave. They called Terry, who came and did in one month what four other carpenters said would take six months to do.

When I saw Terry at the hardware store I asked him if he could put in a screen door for me, the kind that whaps when you close it.

"The kind your grandpa used to have?" he asked.

"That's the one," I told him. Made from big, thick pieces of wood. None of that skinny wood that breaks apart the first time you slam it.

"You want a spring on it?" he asked.

I told him I most certainly did, an honest-to-goodness spring, the kind that pulls tight and fastens to a little hook and catches your leg hair if you're not careful.

"I know just the kind you mean," he said.

A few weeks later I was eating breakfast at the Sunshine Cafe. Terry was there, in the next booth over, enjoying biscuits and gravy.

"I found your door," he told me. "It's big and thick and won't fall apart the first time you slam it. Tom Helton has it up at the Home Lumber. I need to come by and measure your door. Will you be home today?"

He gasped for breath. In all the years I've known Terry, that was the most I'd ever heard him speak at one time.

He came by and looked things over, measured up, down, and across while smoking a cigar. Ordinarily I don't like people smoking on my porch, but I didn't say anything. Having a cigar in his mouth helps Terry think and I wanted his mind keen. A week later the phone rang; it was Terry wanting to know if he could come and hang the door.

It took him four hours. He had to build a frame for the door. He cut the door to fit and chiseled out slots for the hinges. Slow, careful work. Filled in the nail holes and sanded the door. Attached the spring and screwed in the hook and eye. The door stuck a little, so he took it back down and planed the edge. Hung it back up, perfect fit. Then Terry came in, hat in hand, sat at the dining room table, toted up the bill with a nubby pencil, and presented it to me. Two hundred dollars for a thick wood door that whaps shut and four hours' labor. A true bargain.

I've bought a lot of things in my life, but I can't think of one material possession that has brought me more joy than our old-fashioned wood screen door. I sit out on the porch swing on a summer evening, Joan brings me a glass of iced tea, *whap* goes the door, and inwardly I exult. Our boys and various neighborhood children run in and out, *whap* goes the door, and my heart swells with joy. It is a glorious sound, a symphony of wood.

It offers an honest noise, our screen door. The sound of wood on wood, all natural. Lot of fake noise these days. I know a lady who has a machine by her bed that makes cricket noise. It cost her ninety-nine dollars. I feel sorry for people who have to pay ninety-nine dollars to hear a comforting sound. For a hundred more dollars, they could have had an old-fashioned screen door.

Over the years I'd hung a few screen doors on my own. I was going to hang this one, then got to thinking how I owe it to my town to keep good craftsmen in business. Self-sufficiency is fine, but Terry has a family to feed. He needs the money and we need him. For centuries we've subsidized artists and musicians in recognition of their value to a community. We ought to make no less a provision for our craftsmen. That's why I hired Terry to do something I could have done myself. That, and because my wife has seen the doors I've hung and made me hire it done this time.

In my bedroom sits a Shaker rocker. I happened upon it years ago in an antique shop in southern Indiana. It was made in Mount Lebanon, New York, around 1875. How it ended up in southern Indiana is a mystery, but there it was in all its simple glory. A man named Robert Wagan built it. He was a carpenter who joined the Shakers in his adult years, seeking to imbue his life's work with meaning. It wasn't enough for Robert Wagan to build chairs; he wanted to build chairs to the glory of God. Thomas Merton once observed, "The peculiar grace of a Shaker chair is due to the fact that it was made by someone capable of believing that an angel might come and sit on it." Robert Wagan believed that.

Terry hung our door on a Monday, my day off. I sat on the porch swing and watched. It was raining, but the porch is covered and we were dry and content. He charges by the job, not the hour, so he worked slowly, enjoying himself. When the door was hung, he stood back to admire his work, smiling. He also smiled when I paid him, though not as big. I thought how blessed he is to have a job that brings such joy.

Too many people work only for money, a common and foolish mistake. What makes our life's work meaningful is to do it for reasons other than money. After Robert Wagan died, the Shakers started mass-producing chairs to make money. While the chairs were wonderfully crafted, it began their downfall. They needed a better reason to make chairs than money. There are many fine motives for building a chair, but becoming rich is not one of them.

The Shakers had the right idea when they were building chairs for angels to sit on.

CHAPTER NINE

A Time to Weep

Concerning Home Maintenance

Our older son, Spencer, was five years old when we bought our first house. Sam was three. They called it our red house, as in "Are we going to work at the red house today?" or "Are the workers at the red house today?" The word *house* was seldom uttered without the word *work* being tied to it.

Our first meal in the red house was pizza, eaten cold as we sat on packing boxes. We asked Spencer to pray. He bowed his head, clasped his hands, screwed his eyes shut, and intoned, "Give us this day our daily dread." Thus our adventure in home ownership began.

In a letter to some friends, the apostle Paul observed, "Five times I received thirty-nine lashes. Three times I was beaten with sticks; once I was stoned. Three times I was ship-wrecked. Once I was adrift at sea for a day and a half." While I don't wish to minimize the apostle's sufferings, they are child's play compared to my travails. You see, I am a homeowner.

After six months in our home, I wrote my insurance company. "Once my basement has flooded, three times limbs have fallen on my house, twice my dishwasher has broken, and once my pipes burst." I didn't even mention that wind blew my shingles off, my water heater gave out, and my house needed painting. The insurance people were sympathetic. Their letter canceling my policy included a calendar. May features the Grand Canyon, December is a snow-covered New England village, and August pictures a red barn on the Kansas plains. The barn in Kansas needs painting, too. I notice those things now that I'm a homeowner.

The worst tragedy we faced was when our basement flooded. In ten hours we received four inches of rain driven by high winds. A maple tree in Thad Cramer's backyard blew down on top of the electrical wires and knocked out the trunk line, causing our town to lose power for an entire day. Our sump pump shut off and the basement filled with water. If we had been home, I'd have powered up the generator, plugged in the sump pump, and been just fine. But we weren't home; we were at my mother-in-law's working on her house.

Bill Eddy is a plumber in our town and a good friend, despite having punched me in the nose in Mr. Evanoff's fifth-grade class. Consequently, twenty years later I had to have my nose operated on during my vacation time. It was an exceedingly painful experience before, during, and after the operation. But I've managed to put it all behind me. I don't even think about it anymore, except for when it rains and I get intensely throbbing sinus headaches.

When the power went out, Bill called on the phone to check on us but we weren't home. He drove by and looked in our basement window. He told me later, "I knew you had problems when I saw your filing cabinet float by."

Bill went back to his shop for a gas-powered pump and pumped nine thousand gallons of water from our basement in five hours. The average bathtub holds fifty gallons of water. That means we had enough water in our basement to fill 180 bathtubs. Plus there were two frogs. My boys got them.

$\mathcal{I}$n times like these one appreciates good neighbors. Some people stand by noncommittally and observe their neighbors' perils with cool detachment. My neighbors pull on their hip boots and wade right in. Joe Saddler brought his wet/dry vacuum and worked for six hours. His eight-year-old boy, Matthew, worked right alongside us, toting wet pieces of carpet up the stairs and out to the corner. Bill Eddy came that evening with his daughters, Sarah and Melissa, with whom my boys shared their frogs.

As basement floodings go, ours was exceptional. We took a break at dusk and visited on the porch. The rains had stopped and the fields sparkled, as if alight with jewels. We gave Bill the porch swing. He'd pumped out eight basements that day and had earned the privilege. Joe and I sat on lawn chairs. Our wives graced us with iced tea and cherry cobbler while the kids played hide-and-seek. It occurred to me, sitting there in that sweet moment, that this was the second generation of children to play together.

Thirty years ago, Bill and Joe and I played

the same games in the same little town. I'm glad to be back here, flooded basement and all. Some things have changed in the twenty years I was away. Joe's daddy is gone, and Bill's father with him. 1981 and 1993, respectively. I spoke the words over Bill's father at the graveyard. George Eddy was a guidance counselor and a wood-worker. Every time I saw him, he had sawdust in his hair. To this day, I have an inherent respect for men with sawdust in their hair.

My father is the lone survivor. The night we were cleaning the basement, he was there. To supervise, he said, though his orders were few. The year before he'd had a heart attack and a quadruple bypass. His edge is gone. Nothing flusters him anymore, not even wet basements. I would have a wet basement once a week if it meant spending more time with my father. He cheated the reaper by one artery. Having almost lost him, I treasure his presence more than ever.

Bill and Joe have a father hunger. Not a day passes when they don't think of their daddies. They ease the loss by doting on their mothers. They are good sons and good friends.

The morning of my father's operation, my brothers and sister and mother gathered in his hospital room. After a while the doctor came in and said they were ready for surgery. We prayed a prayer and filed out of the room. I was the last to leave, and when I did Dad called me back in. He lifted up the Gideon Bible from beside his bed, pulled out a piece of paper, and handed it to me. "Just in case," he told me. I opened the paper and read it. They were his burial instructions, penned during a sleepless night. He went over his instructions, line by line. "I want to be buried at the South Cemetery. Have Bob Bales pick the grave site. He knows where the best spots are. I want you to give the eulogy. If you're not able, ask Pastor Thornburg at the Quaker meeting."

I folded the paper and put it in my pocket. This was a conversation I had never rehearsed and never expected to have. As a pastor, I had many conversations like this, but never with my father. Whenever we eat out together my dad always pays the check. If I reach for the bill, he slaps my hand away and says it's a father's joy to care for his son. Now it was my turn to care for him. Full circle. But it didn't bring me joy.

They wheeled Dad away. Six hours later the doctor came out, a smile on his face. An hour later we got to see Dad, and five days after that Dad came home. The doctors were optimistic.

No more red meat or cigarettes, they told him. He agreed and pledged his promise on the Gideon Bible. I took his burial instructions and put them in my desk under glass. Every time I open my top right-hand drawer, I'm faced with my father's mortality. I'm no longer a little boy thinking my daddy will live forever. I'm a man with sons of my own coming to understand how frayed are the cords which bind us to this earth.

A few days after our basement flooded, the insurance man stopped by. We were his sixth basement that day, and he was weary. Joan served him iced tea and cherry cobbler and took him to the back porch swing. I told him of Bill pumping out the water, of Joe coming with his wet/dry vacuum, of my near-miss father supervising the operation, of children playing hide-and-seek when the storm had passed and the fields were alight with jewels. As flooded basements go, I told him, ours was exceptional.

With the insurance money I bought a new washer and dryer, a water heater, and a dehumidifier. I was left with eighty dollars. I'm thinking of taking Joe, Bill, and Dad to dinner. Joe, Bill, and I can have steaks. Dad can have baked chicken. When we moved into our house, if someone had mentioned the benefits of flooded basements I would have thought it absurd. Now I am learning that blessings, like water, can flow from any corner.

CHAPTER TEN

A Time to Laugh

Sandlot Baseball

My father was a Little League coach when I was growing up. He coached the Printer's Devils, which was sponsored by the local newspaper, *The Republican*. A printer's devil was an apprentice who worked for a newspaper learning the trade. That catchy phrase isn't used anymore because newspapers no longer employ apprentices. Journalists today learn their trade in college. Newspapers were better when journalists learned how to write from wizened old men who smoked cigars and swore like sailors.

Betty Weesner owned *The Republican* and still does. She inherited it from her father, Pug Weesner. *The Republican* first rolled off the presses in 1847 and hasn't missed an issue since. Betty Weesner prays every day someone will come along and take over after she's gone. I walk by her office, just east of the courthouse, and see her bent over the old Linotype. Sometimes I think of walking through her door and asking if she'll take me on as a printer's devil and teach me that wonderful trade.

My father coached thirty years ago, when it cost one hundred dollars to sponsor a Little League team. That bought twelve uniforms. The kids had to buy their shoes and mitts and the coach paid for the trip to the Dairy Queen if the team won. Betty would bring her lawn chair to each game, unfold it next to the dugout, and oversee her investment.

In addition to Betty Weesner, the two banks each sponsored a team, along with Baker's Hardware, Stevenson-Jensen Insurance, and the Home Lumber Company. There were a few other teams whose names now escape me. This was, after all, thirty years ago. What I remember is Betty Weesner sitting in her lawn chair cheering on her boys. Girls didn't play back then.

I played for Baker's Hardware under Coach Buck Leath. The highlight of my career was when Buck's son, Jeff, got hit by a line drive and Buck nodded at me to take his place on the pitcher's mound. I pitched a no-hitter. Walked twelve straight batters. Mostly I played right field, in front of the Meazel's Jewelers sign. *Jewelry for the Discriminating Customer,* the sign read. The out-field fence was lined with signs from local establishments. I was not kept very busy in right field and by season's end had all the signs mem-orized, in order, starting with Max Poynter Insurance and ending with Johnston's Regal Grocery—*Why Shop Anywhere Else? For Home Delivery, Dial Sherwood 5-4285.*

All of this took place in the late 1960s and early 1970s, before parents were so earnest and everything became a big production. Parents would sit on the bleachers and visit, unless it was their turn to work the concession stand, where they sold licorice whips for a penny and orange Push-Ups for a dime. The children played underneath the stands and told jokes. "Say, did you hear about the book, *Under the Bleachers*, by Seymour Bottoms?" You could hear them cackle.

There was a game every June evening except for Sundays and Wednesdays, which were church nights. The game began after supper at seven o'clock. At 7:45, Joe Hawkins threw the switch up in the crow's nest and light would flood the field. If you tired of the game, you could watch the bugs under the lights. If you were especially lucky, Joe Hawkins might pick you to sit on the scoreboard and hang the numbers at the end of each inning.

People didn't take the games very seriously. Occasionally a coach might get upset and yell. Once I remember my normally calm father unbuckling his Timex wristwatch and flinging it toward the outfield. After the game he sent me to look for it, but I couldn't find it. The watch had been a birthday gift from my mother, who gave him a porch swing the next year, reasoning that it couldn't be as easily thrown.

They still play Little League at the park. Joe Hawkins still throws the light switch at 7:45 P.M. and still picks the kids to run the scoreboard. I take my sons to the park to watch. They can't tell the difference between Little League games, which are free, and Indianapolis Indians games, which are not, so I take them to Little League games. Not much has changed over the years except that the parents seem a little more uptight, as if their family pride is on the line.

Little League championships are now televised. Teams from Japan play teams from Puerto Rico. Major league scouts lurk in the stands, hoping to spot the next Mark McGwire. Shoe manufacturers pass out free shoes, wanting to embed their logo in the minds of impressionable youth. This confirms my worst suspicion about organized sports—that given the chance, adults will eventually taint any sport in which they have a part.

I have read of enraged Little League parents fighting and cursing and storming the umpire. Parents gone berserk. Red-faced, vein-popping, eye-bulging mad. There is a certain father in the local soccer league who screams at his five-year-old son to "go on the attack" and "stop messing around." One Saturday morning, I watched the fifteen-year-old referee stop the game and escort the man to the parking lot. It thrilled me to no end. I was happy the rest of the day.

My older son plays in the soccer league. I was opposed to it at the time and still am. I'm skeptical of any enterprise where the adults keep asking the children if they're having fun. I don't go out of my way to attend every game, nor do I make him practice with me every day in the yard so he'll have an edge. I believe children are better served when adults have their games and children have theirs. I do want him to play sports, so I bought a house with a big yard. But I want him to play with children, not adults. If I'm not careful I could be a real crackpot about this.

When I was growing up, I played sandlot baseball, which is now in its death throes. This is because parents don't want children to organize their own play, for fear that children chosen last will be scarred for life. I played sandlot ball every summer day and was invariably chosen last. If I had run home crying about it, my mother would have swatted me on the bottom and sent me back to the Barrys' front yard, which is where we played. The stump from the maple tree was first base, the tulip tree second base, the lilac bush third base. Home plate was Kevin Barry's T-shirt.

Not everyone had a baseball mitt, so we shared. No one had cleats, though my brother Doug once taped thumbtacks to the bottom of his Keds tennis shoes. We played ten innings or until someone came up with a better game to play or until James Martin had to leave and take his ball with him. Never once did a parent intrude, offering to pitch or help choose sides or umpire. We would have thought it absurd and quickly found something else to do. Adults, after all, were strange creatures, to be avoided at all costs.

This was back in the days when children had huge chunks of summer hours to fill, back when parents didn't feel the need to cram every hour with meaningful activity. So we swam in the creek, rode our bikes all over town, and played sandlot baseball, girls and boys alike. Carol Barry was a good batter, had an arm like Willie Mays, and could run like the wind. When we entered Little League and the adults told us girls couldn't play, it only confirmed our suspicions that adults were stranger than strange. Of course, we knew girls were different but we didn't know the difference, though we suspected it had something to do with Carol Barry's never offering her shirt for home plate.

Ours was not a precise game. It was roughly thirty feet from home plate to first base, but nearly twice as far from first base to second, which made hitting a double an occasion for pride. We had no umpire. If the catcher tagged you out at home plate and you thought you were safe, you argued for five minutes then reached a suitable compromise. No adult intervened. No parent hastened out to see what all the noise was about. It was glorious fun.

Certain Christians I know are suspicious of fun. They live in constant fear that someone, somewhere, is having a good time. They believe faith is a serious, somber business. Jesus never subscribed to that notion. He told his followers, "In the world you have tribulation; but be of good cheer, I have overcome the world." When we live as if that isn't true, when even fun is serious business, we pollute the gospel. We're like those Little League parents who've turned a harvest of joy into a plague of misery. For further reading on this topic, please see *Under the Bleachers* by Seymour Bottoms.

CHAPTER ELEVEN

A Time to Mourn

The Gravedigger

Our house sits atop Joe Stevenson's old horse farm, north of town. It's tucked amidst a creek and a pond and sixty acres of trees Mrs. Forest Blanton donated to our town on condition they never be bulldozed.

Nature assaults our house relentlessly. I spend considerable time defending my homestead against forest, water, wind, and sun. There are fence rows to clean, trees to trim, clapboards to paint, and a basement to keep dry. Thus far, victory is mine, just barely. Our house was built on top of an underground spring, a common occurrence in these parts. When the basement was being dug, they diverted the spring into our sump pit. The sump pump carries the water out to the storm drain. An engineering marvel.

In the rainy season, you can hear the water falling into the sump pit. The tinkling of the water stimulates my kidneys, so I resolved to fix it. I called Walter. He is the man in our town you hire if you need a hole dug. If you want to hook up to the town sewer system, you call Walter and he comes out in his backhoe, digs the trench, and lays the pipe. Then he puts the dirt back, smooths it out, rakes in some grass seed, covers it with straw, and spreads netting to keep the straw from blowing away. Walter has been at this work for years. He is a good man to know. When he came to my house he told me he could dig a hole and pipe the underground spring away from my house and into the creek. Walter assures me it will soothe my kidneys, so I'm considering it.

In addition to trenches, Walter digs our graves. The day before a burial he digs the hole and covers it with plywood. Next day, a half hour before the funeral, he comes back and removes the plywood. Then he walks about fifty yards away and leans against a tree while the funeral procession threads its way through the cemetery. The mourners climb from their cars and trudge over to the burial site. Walter waits underneath the tree until the minister has spoken, the people have left, and the undertaker has taken down the funeral tent. Then he fills the hole, rakes in grass seed, covers it with straw, and spreads netting so the straw won't blow away.

*A*ll the funerals in Danville are held at ten in the morning. By 10:45 the grievers are at the cemetery and by 11:15 they are getting back in their cars and returning to their church for a luncheon in the basement. Except for Walter—who fills and tends the grave, then drives to the Sunshine Cafe where he eats lunch and wonders who is going to dig his grave when the Lord calls him home. He worries about that. Walter believes his Bible when it comes to bodily resurrection—that when Jesus returns, the dead in Christ will rise and the graveyards will empty. Consequently, he doesn't like to bury people too deep. He doesn't want them to stir to life on that glorious morning and have to struggle through six feet of Indiana clay. So he buries people at five feet. He is worried that whoever digs his grave might go too deep and there he'd be, stuck in the ground on Glory Day.

Walter hopes he'll have advance notice of his death, so he can dig his own grave before he succumbs. His worst fear is that he will die unexpectedly in his sleep. He wants just enough time to fire up his backhoe, drive to the cemetery, and dig his own grave. He has made a dry run. He needs two hours, tops. He lies in bed at night and prays, "Dear Lord, if you could be so kind as to warn me of my death, I would be grateful. Two hours, Lord, that's all I need." Then he falls asleep, peace in his heart.

Walter buried his own mother—a kind and godly woman. It was his best grave ever—the walls straight, the grave a shallow four feet. When she rises from her grave, he doesn't want her to break a sweat. She worked hard all her life and he doesn't want her to have to labor on Glory Day. Walter wept as he dug her grave, his tears cleaving a shiny path down his dusty face. The next day, after the mourners were gone, he climbed atop his backhoe in his brown suit and filled her grave. He cried then, too.

For two summers my brother David tended the cemetery, steering the Cub Cadet tractor up and down the solemn rows. Long pants, shirt tucked in, clean cap, washed behind the ears.

This is our sacred burial ground, our Golgotha, our place of skulls, and we don't profane it with sloppy dress and dirty ears. My brother says when Walter is finished filling a grave, the ground is glass-smooth. Twenty-two acres and not a bump anywhere, David reports. A sterling endorsement.

In some towns, the Catholics and Protestants separate their dead. In our town, we share the stores, the schools, and the cemetery. Neighbors in life, neighbors in death. In the southeast corner we bury our children. Angels adorn the tombstones. Teddy bears appear from time to time, mostly in the spring and on the anniversary of a child's death. Children who would be forty years old, had they lived, still get teddy bears. The workers are under strict orders: do not mow over the teddy bears. Pick them up, mow, put them back. A gentle seemliness pervades the twenty-two acres.

We do not frown upon mourning in our town. We do not encourage people to set aside their sorrow and get on with their lives, a peculiarly modern tendency promoted by a society afraid of tears. In our town, we respect grief. There are widows who, on the tenth anniversary of their husbands' passing, receive cards and flowers and get mentioned at church prayer time. We bow our heads and pray for hearts not healed after ten long years. We are not morbid, but we do take death seriously here. It is a good place to be buried.

If Jesus lingers and we abide in these earthen graves a little longer than we planned, we will be well cared for. The words spoken over us will be hushed and polite. The grass over us, clipped and lush. And because Walter doesn't bury us too deep, we will not have to struggle on Glory Day.

Walter is my inspiration. What he lacks in theological sophistication he makes up for in grace. Dealing as he does with those who mourn, he has become an exceedingly tender man. I do not know if first he was gentle and thus drawn to a ministry of consolation, or if years of funeral watching have softened his heart. I only know that he is kind, that his tears have dampened many a grave. I consider it a mystery how mourning can turn some people soft and others hard. I am acquainted with certain persons whose grief immersed them in the holy. But I know others whose suffering tore a spiritual cleft between them and the Divine, folks whose faith died right along with their loved one. Sometimes when we most need faith it seems to flee into the night.

Walter believes the only thing that can come between us and God is five feet of Indiana clay. I wish that were so. Pride and greed and self-righteousness dig their chasms, too. But of all the things that keep our hearts from God, grief might erect the most obstinate barrier—the stubborn, clinging belief that God is not for us, that his love has cooled, his heart turned hard.

But time after time, tear after tear, Jesus Christ proves otherwise. "Come to me, all who labor and are heavy laden, and I will give you rest." The Greek word used for *rest* also means "refreshment." Walter doesn't know Greek. But he does know refreshment. And if, on burying day, you share lunch with him at the Sunshine Cafe, he'll tell you from whence it comes.

CHAPTER TWELVE

A Time to Dance

The Pastor's Short Course

When Quakerism was launched in 1650, its founders were suspicious of paid preachers. Hirelings, they called them, who took pay for doing something God-fearing Christians ought to do for free. Nobody ever gave Jesus a paycheck, they said. After 250 years of toeing the line, we caved in and began paying pastors. If I weren't a pastor, I would oppose it too. But since I am one, I can offer any number of reasons why pastors ought to be paid.

The decision to pay pastors was a contentious one, with some Quakers for it and others opposed. They compromised by paying us, just not very much. The first four years of my ministry I received forty dollars a week and tithed fifty—a losing proposition. Nevertheless, I stuck with the pastoral ministry for fourteen years because I loved the work and because if I weren't a pastor I couldn't attend the annual Quaker Pastor's Short Course, which is held every February at Turkey Run State Park Inn.

I don't know how the Pastor's Short Course came by its name. When I first learned of it, I reasoned that there must also be a Pastor's Long Course, but there isn't and never was. The Short Course is all we get, that and forty dollars a week. The Quaker Pastor's Short Course lasts for two nights and three days. It starts at one o'clock in the afternoon, a sneaky way of not having to feed us lunch. On the closing day, they push us out the door at eleven o'clock in the morning, once again robbing us of our noonday meal.

The purpose of the Pastor's Short Course, according to the pastor's handbook, is to provide the pastor further opportunities for education, fellowship, and spiritual growth. A committee of people who never attended the Pastor's Short Course came up with that. The same committee hires a speaker every year, an expert on church growth or Bible study or something of that nature—whatever the committee perceives we need.

One year the committee brought in a semi-nary professor who, to our delight, preached union doctrine and had us singing solidarity songs such as "We Shall Overcome" and "This Land Is Your Land." For a few wild days we thought of striking, of holing up at Turkey Run State Park Inn until our demands for better working conditions were met: higher pay and fewer meetings. This wasn't what the committee had in mind, so they never asked the seminary professor back, and we're still making forty dollars a week. But for three glorious days the world was ours.

The next year they brought in a speaker who talked for three days about the joys of ministry and how no amount of money could compare to the joy of serving the Lord. He promised us riches in heaven for our faithful labors here below. My friend Stan Banker raised his hand and asked if he could have his riches early. Stan has been a pastor for twenty-five years. His chief regret is that God didn't call him to the Episco-palian faith, where priests clean up, according to

Stan. His goal is to be the first Quaker pastor to become a millionaire on forty dollars a week. He subscribes to *Money* magazine and can name the top ten mutual funds at any given time. After twenty-five years, Stan is halfway to his goal. His word to the wise: *dollar-cost averaging!* Take that forty dollars a week, put it in a mutual fund, and leave it there.

One year at Pastor's Short Course a man from the Quaker headquarters talked with us about financial planning, retirement, and health insurance. His advice was succinct. Regarding financial planning—arrange to be named in a will. Concerning retirement—Wal-Mart can always use new greeters. In regards to health insurance—don't get sick. Sound advice.

*A*rdith Stands has attended most every Pastor's Short Course since 1959. She is the widow of Blaine Stands, a pastor who died of bone cancer in 1988. That was the year Ardith missed the Pastor's Short Course. I once asked her if she had a favorite Pastor's Short Course, one that stuck in her memory. She told about the year the furnace broke and the Turkey Run State Park Inn management wanted to send all the pastors to the hotel in Rockville. The pastors told them not to bother, that they lived in Quaker parsonages and were accustomed to broken furnaces.

"That was a good year," Ardith said. "We felt right at home."

Ardith is especially fond of Talent Night, which is held the last night of the Pastor's Short Course. The word *talent* is interpreted loosely. I do an impersonation of Chester on *Gunsmoke*. Bill Kinsey recites Victorian poetry. Don Perry sings a gospel hymn. Catherine Sherman displays her needlework. George Freer demonstrates his train collection and Ann Carter reads her essay about caskets, which is the highlight of the whole affair. We save it for last. We end the night with a dance. Helen Johnson brings numerous musical tapes and a boom box. We don't call it a dance, not caring to offend the sensibilities of those Quakers opposed to dance. We list it in the program as "Devotion in Motion."

The chairs are pushed back to the wall. The piano is rolled to the corner. We are awkward dancers; Helen advises removing our shoes to prevent damage to our partners' insteps. Our socks are clean. We have learned, after these many years, to slip back to our rooms after supper and don fresh socks. We stand in a circle, toes a-wiggle, holding hands. Helen stands in the middle, calling the steps. At first, rhythm eludes us. There is an abundance of bumping, murmured apologies, half-steps, missteps, and studiously watched feet. By the third song, we are acquiring grace. Less bumping, faces raised, humming and soft singing. By the fifth song, our movements are like poetry. We could now wear shoes without injuring our partners, but we leave them off, not wanting to disrupt the magic.

There comes a moment when the dance is perfect. I watch my wife laugh and spin and sing, her face aglow. I remember then why I fell in love with her. I wonder why we don't do this more often. I resolve to remedy that, to find a baby-sitter and steal away for an evening of dance, though the evening never comes. One obligation or another keeps me from it—meetings to attend, persons to counsel, sermons to write. I haven't the courage to say to one of my flock, "I'm sorry, I can't meet with you tonight. I'm going dancing," even though Ecclesiastes advises a time for it.

Our children attend Pastor's Short Course. They have their own program except on Dance Night, when we join together. Other hotel guests wander in to watch, lured by the music. They stare, bewildered, wondering who we are. A few of them, I can tell, ache to dance with us. Would love to tug off their shoes and join our circle, which we would welcome, though they never do. They always appear to me as people who could use the joy. I wonder what keeps them from it. Perhaps a voice in their heads, cautioning, scolding, admonishing them not to make fools of themselves. A voice from their past, warning against any and all frivolity. A grim, snapping voice. A few of the pastors know that voice and sit on the perimeter, their shoes tightly laced and their faces tight and dour. I know them well, these pastors. Sour, somber people trying to preach a gospel of freshness and vitality. Persons of death preaching a gospel of life. It makes no sense to me.

Ardith Stands isn't one for the sidelines. She's a dancer, right in the thick of it, every year since 1959. Except 1988, which was her time to mourn. But she was back the next year, circling with the rest of us. There is a time to mourn, and a time to dance. Life provides ample opportunity for mourning. It's the dancing that comes hard to us, the spinning and singing with faces aglow.

On the first anniversary of my passing, I want Helen Johnson to come with her music tapes and boom box. No shoes allowed. Children are welcome. Sourpusses are not.

CHAPTER THIRTEEN

A Time to Cast Away Stones

Vanity of Vanities, All is Vanity

When I was in my early thirties, I received a phone call inviting me to serve on the executive committee of a national Quaker organization. It was an important committee staffed with bright, accomplished people, and I was honored to be asked, though mystified why I had been chosen. When I went to the first meeting, the other committee members looked at me with some confusion. Several commented that I looked remarkably young for my age. I smiled and thanked them, speaking in as deep a voice as I could muster.

I found out later that an error had been

made. A man with the same last name as mine, a retired college president, was the one nominated to the committee, but the person doing the phoning had mistakenly called my number, which appeared just beneath their intended nominee's number in the Quaker directory. By the time they realized their mistake, they were too embarrassed to un-ask me, so there I was, sitting on the executive committee of a national Quaker organization.

It was glorious fun, and the knowledge that I wasn't their intended choice didn't dampen my enthusiasm a bit. Four times a year they flew me somewhere for three days of meetings, sightseeing, and visiting with other Quakers. I saw New England in autumn, Arizona in February, the New Mexico highlands, historic Philadelphia, and the pueblos of San Juan. On my journeys I met a podiatrist, the parents of a Mexican presidential candidate, and the man who owns the largest doughnut factory in the Midwest. All good people to know if I ever have foot trouble, decide to enter Mexican politics, or hunger for a doughnut.

But that wasn't the best part of serving on the executive committee of a national Quaker

organization. The best part was *telling my friends*
that I served on the executive committee of a
national Quaker organization. For three years I
lived in the hope that someone would ask me to
do something on a weekend I was scheduled to
be traveling for the committee. Then I could say,
"Oh, I would love to come to your house for
dinner, but I'll be in Philadelphia that weekend
with the executive committee of a national
Quaker organization." I would smile modestly
as I said it, relishing their raised eyebrows and
heightened respect.

The last time I felt so important was in 1972
when I won second place in the Danville
Optimist Bicycle Safety Rodeo. Randy White
won first place and a new bicycle from Floyd's
Bicycle Shop. I won second place and twenty-
five dollars. Kevin Barry won third place and ten
dollars. This was serious money in 1972.

The girls had a separate bicycle safety rodeo.
Sherri Bishop, whom I secretly loved, won second place. For years afterward, I hoped our
common victory might bring us together, that
we understood each other in ways others could
not. On the night of our high school graduation,

when we attended the same party, I drew next to her, hoping she would whisper in my ear, "Phil, I've loved you ever since 1972."

But the only thing she said was, "Why are you standing so close to me?" Then she moved away and I haven't seen her since, though I think of her every May when I open *The Republican* newspaper and see the winners of the annual Danville Optimist Bicycle Safety Rodeo. I get a faraway look in my eyes and my wife asks me what I'm thinking about. "Nothing," I tell her, "nothing at all." Everyone has a secret and that is mine.

The reason these honors mean so much to me is because I have always felt the need to be well thought of. I want other people to like me, to admire me. I cherish the good opinion of others. It is my weakness, my failing, that I care too much what others think of me. Consequently, I sometimes exaggerate my accomplishments in order that others might admire me even more.

When I first stumbled upon Ecclesiastes, I did not know what it meant to cast away stones and why we should make a time for it. After hours of research, which consisted mostly of eating biscuits and gravy with my friend Jim at the Bob Evans Restaurant, I discovered that casting away stones had to do with tearing down altars erected to idols. In the Bible, idols were those objects that represented devotion to a false god. In those days the sure way to get zapped by God was to worship an idol.

*T*oday we still have idols, and they're more sophisticated than mere graven images. Modern idols are those things we love more than God, including the obvious temptations like cars, fancy houses, and grand- sounding job titles. But we also idolize certain other things we've been taught to count supreme—good things like country and family and one's reputation. If we value anything more than God, it is idolatry, plain and simple. When I care more about the good opinion of others than I do about God, I am an idolater, guilty of honoring self above God.

Idolatry, it pains me to say, is a sin. A whopper of a sin, according to the Old Testament. It kept Moses from setting foot in the Promised Land. Idolatry caused the prophets of Baal to be roasted in a fire. The warning against idolatry was number one in the Top Ten Rules: "You shall have no other gods before me." In Exodus, God stipulated the punishment for idol worshipers: utter destruction. This was back when God was not the mellow, fair-minded deity we've come to know and love, before all that New Testament talk about grace and forgiveness.

To be accurate, despite our indifference to idolatry, God still gets his dander up about it. God is funny that way. He wants to be first in our lives, not for the sake of his ego but for the sake of our joy. Thus, he commands his followers to worship God and God alone. Because all other gods, these little g gods, ultimately disappoint. They are straw gods who wither when life heats up. So it is for our joy that God commands our devotion. God alone is the one who is forever faithful, who never disappoints, whose love knows no end.

Our money won't last. Our houses will rot and be gone. Our jobs will move south. Our country will err. Our families will fracture. Our reputations can change with one sin or one slur. But the King of kings, the Rock of Ages, the Eternal Lover, is the Friend who never leaves, the Song that never stops, the Father whose door is always open, the Mother who gathers, guides, and guards her children.

In all my years as a pastor I never met a

worshiper of Baal, though I ran across idolatry
most every day. I saw it in others; I saw it in
myself. I saw it when people yearned for money
over holiness. I saw it when people chose pres-
tige over humility. I saw it when people picked
religion over relationship. These are the stones
we ought to cast aside, the altars we need to tear
down. It is easier said than done, this loving
God above all else, but it can be done.

I see it in pastors who shun rich pulpits to
minister to the poor and broken. I see it in parents who teach their children to esteem the
rejected and despised. I see it in persons who
yearn not for the approval of their neighbors,
but only for God's "Well done, thou good and
faithful servant." We can love God above all else.
It is possible. I have seen it done. It is simply a
matter of knowing which stones to cast away
and which altars to tear down.

My service on the executive committee came
to an end, and with it my honor. Floyd's Bicycle
Shop closed. Sherri Bishop married someone
else. Vanity of vanities, all is vanity.

CHAPTER FOURTEEN

A Time to Gather Stones Together

On Patios and Porches

I'm a prejudiced person, which over the years has saved me a great deal of trouble.

For instance, I can pretty well predict that if two people carrying Bibles knock on my door, they are Jehovah's Witnesses and I'm better off quieting the children and pretending no one's home. If the phone rings at supper time and a lady asks, "May I please speak with Mr. Gulley?" I know it's a telephone solicitor. I tell her Mr. Gulley suffered a horrible accident, that he was hurled through the air while riding a roller coaster and is unable to come to the phone at this time. Usually this ends the conversation. These are prejudices that make life easier.

These aren't my only prejudices; I have others. It's been my experience that people who have front porches are open and honest and don't fear scrutiny. People with back porches are furtive and sneaky and are trying to hide something from their neighbors. That's why they hide behind their houses.

Most new houses don't have front porches. People sit on wood decks out back. This is because people today are less honest than they used to be. George Washington, Abraham Lincoln, and Harry Truman had houses with front porches. Richard Nixon and Bill Clinton had back porches.

My next-door neighbors are honest people. I know that because they have a front porch. People drive by and wave and think, *Those Halls are such nice people!* Then they pass my house and catch a glimpse of me on the back porch swing. *What's he doing back there?* they wonder.

Wanting to upgrade my reputation, I considered building a front porch on my house. I decided against it, because my house just doesn't lend itself to a front porch. If you put a front porch on a house that isn't intended to have one, it looks as if you're putting on a false front, like a used-car salesman carrying a Bible. Instead I decided to build a stone patio on the side of my house. Right out in the open. An honest man, with nothing to hide.

There are two different ways to build a stone patio—the right way and the wrong way. The right way is to dig down six inches, then tamp the earth level. Pour a concrete border. Dump down four inches of pea gravel, spread it smooth, then put two inches of sand on top of that. Rake the sand level, then fit the stones together so the tops are slightly above ground level and water won't pool. If you want sand between the stones, you sweep it in between the joints. If you want mortar between the joints, which you do, then sweep in dry concrete, hose it down, and let it set for a day before walking on it. This involves a great deal of work, which proves that people with stone patios are not only industrious but full of virtue.

The wrong way to build a stone patio is to buy a load of stones and arrange them on top of the ground. It isn't as much work, but your chairs will wobble and the cold weather will cause the stones to heave. Grass will sprout between the cracks and in a few years you'll have to tear the patio out and build it right. It's cheaper to build a wood patio, though wood doesn't last as long, needs more maintenance, and gives you splinters. A well-built stone patio will outlast you and the maple tree you plant alongside it for shade.

Arlene Pease lives south of me, on the road to town. I go to visit and we sit on a stone patio her husband built in 1940. It shows no sign of fading. Its only concession to age is the moss that grows in the cracks between the stones. When Mrs. Pease turned ninety-five, she thought of moving to a retirement home. But the retirement home had a wood patio and Mrs. Pease couldn't abide that. "I wonder what else they cut corners on," she observed.

Once you've had a stone patio, you're not likely to settle for anything less. While you can use almost any kind of stone to make a stone patio, the best stone to use is Pennsylvania bluestone. I don't know why they call it that, because it isn't blue, it's gray. But if you want a nice patio, that's the stone to use. Some people, when building a stone patio, use six-sided bricks called pavers. This is a matter of personal preference, though people who use pavers instead of

Pennsylvania bluestone tend toward laziness and don't believe in God. This is a prejudice of mine that over time has proven correct more often than not. There is another big difference between Pennsylvania bluestone and brick pavers. Pennsylvania bluestone was handmade by God on the second day of Creation for the express purpose of giving us a cool place to sit, drink our iced tea, and wave to our neighbors. Brick pavers are made in New Jersey by the mafia, who use the proceeds to buy drugs and make dirty movies. I think you need to be aware of the difference so you can make an informed decision.

A big mistake people make when building a stone patio is putting it in the wrong place. You need to live in your house at least a year before building your stone patio. By then it will be clear where it needs to go. If your next-door neighbor has a loud teenager, you want your stone patio on the other side of the house, where it's peaceful. You want it close to the kitchen door, so when you run out of iced tea it takes no effort to refill your glass.

If you don't have shade on your patio, plant trees without delay. It might be too late to do you any good, but the people after you will

appreciate your thoughtfulness. Elton True-
blood wrote in *The Life We Prize,* "A man has
made at least a start on discovering the meaning
of human life when he plants shade trees under
which he knows full well he will never sit." He
wrote that while sitting on a stone patio in England. When you sit on a stone patio, wise
sayings fairly roll off your tongue.

There are people who build stone patios for
a living, but you should try to build it yourself.
Some people will claim they don't have the time
to build their own stone patio, but if you have
the time to sit on a patio, you have the time to
build it. Most of us hire our houses built, which
robs us of the deep satisfaction of creating something enduring with our own hands. Building
your own stone patio provides that satisfaction.

Then people come to visit and say, "My, that's
a lovely stone patio. Who built it?"

You smile modestly. "Well, I did, but it was
nothing."

They stand back to admire the crisp lines,
the level stones, the moss in the cracks, the
shade from the maple tree you planted. The
whole picture. It is a fine moment. Had you paid
someone to build it for you, the feeling wouldn't
be nearly as sweet.

There is a joy in creating that is unmatched by any other joy. A contentment which mounts as board is nailed to board, stone is stacked on stone, or one patch is quilted to another. A slow and rising joy. I imagine this is God's joy as he fashions his creation one child, one songbird, one flower at a time. It is enough to make you glow, to know there is a God in heaven who delights in you, who gazes with quiet love at what he has fashioned. To know his love is forever present. Nothing—not one thing, Scripture boldly declares—can separate us from the love of God. It is the love of a Creator enthralled with his creation.

I might be prejudiced, but I believe God even loves people with back porches, despite the fact that we're furtive and sneaky and try to hide things from our neighbors. I've even heard it told that God has a soft spot for telephone solicitors. Now if that isn't grace, I don't know what is.

CHAPTER FIFTEEN

A Time to Embrace

A Preschool Meditation

When our older son, Spencer, turned five, we sent him to preschool. We had begun a preschool at our Quaker meeting but got bogged down in committee meetings and things ground to a halt. When people tell me they're tired of organized religion, I invite them to become Quakers.

Can't remember now why we wanted a Quaker preschool. I think it was because we didn't believe anyone outside our small Quaker circle could care for our children as we did. But ventures born of mistrust seldom succeed, and ours was no exception. After three meetings, we threw in the towel and took our children to the Methodist preschool.

Each of the preschool classes was named for an animal. There was the Butterflies class. Butterflies possess a quiet beauty. Like birds, they migrate thousands of miles, returning to the same place each year. Beautiful, with a keen sense of direction. What an honor to be a Butterfly! Then there was the Bears class. Bears are strong and mighty creatures. The children who marched into the Bears classroom did so with pride. Spencer was assigned to the Turtles class. Turtles are plodders and they tinkle on your hand when you hold them. Our son is not a plodder, and he has never tinkled on our hands. Still, it could have been worse. They could have put him in the Slugs class.

Joan and I went with him on his first day. We took our camera to take pictures. His hair was slicked back, his shirt tucked in. New shoes. Mickey Mouse backpack. It was chaotic. I've never heard such crying and carrying on. But after a while I settled down and things were fine.

Despite our fears, Spencer's first day of preschool went well. He learned about the letter *A* and how to write it. He showed me his paper.

He had written *Aa, Aa, Aa*...all the way across his paper. People say how everything has changed, but I'm pleased to report they're still making *A*'s the same way they used to.

*T*here were twenty children in the Turtles class and two teachers, Mrs. Campbell and Mrs. Griffin. I never learned their first names. Do teachers even have first names? I would see them at the grocery store and say, "Hello, Mrs. Griffin" or "How are you, Mrs. Campbell?" I liked them both. When I picked up Spencer, they would whisper in my ear, "Your son is our best student." I wonder if they said that to all the fathers.

One autumn night, the Turtles class had a hayride and wiener roast. I told Joan I was busy and couldn't go; I had made plans to polish my shoes that night. Boy, was she mad. She said when you're a parent, sometimes you have to sacrifice your own desires for the good of the kids. So I ended up going on the hayride. I'm glad I got my sacrifice out of the way early.

In between Thanksgiving and Christmas they practiced a Christmas pageant. It was held the Sunday before Christmas, during church.

The place was packed—parents, grandparents, friends, and neighbors. When all the animals had shuffled in, the angel of the Lord rose to speak. "Behold, I bring you good news of a great joy which will come to all the people; for to you is born this day in the city of David a Savior, who is Christ the Lord." I've heard that verse a thousand times and its beauty still leaves me breathless.

Spencer graduated from preschool with honors. The uprights on his letters were arrow-straight, which won him the honor of bearing the flag at the preschool graduation held in the basement of the Methodist church. Mrs. Campbell and Mrs. Griffin were there, beaming and kissing cheeks. When my son's name was called and he strode across the stage with his hair slicked back and shirt tucked in, I swelled with pride. *My boy is going places,* I thought to myself.

Where he went was to kindergarten. Mrs. Fruits's afternoon class. For the first week he couldn't remember her name and kept calling her Mrs. Plum. Mrs. Fruits has been at it for thirty years. Her former students see her in the grocery store and say, "Hello, Mrs. Fruits.

How are you?" No one knows her first name. My son is enamored with her. While the other children play outside, he sits at the kitchen table and draws pictures of cowboys, excavators, and whales—all for Mrs. Fruits.

Mrs. Fruits has three rules: no talking out of turn, no poking other children, and no changing seats. Violators get their name written on the chalkboard. Every day when Spencer comes home, I take him in my lap, look stern, and ask him in a somber voice if his name was written on the chalkboard. He tells me no and I hug him. I haven't figured out what I'll do if he ever answers yes.

Spencer's best friend at school is Sam Headley, who is some sort of marvel. All through dinner Spencer talks about Sam Headley. "Sam Headley guessed what was in the surprise box today. Sam Headley was the line leader today. Shelly Neilson called Sam Headley her sweet baboo." I've never met Sam Headley and can scarcely wait.

One day the school nurse, Mrs. Edmondson, called. Spencer was sick. Could I come? He had lost a tooth, tasted blood, and vomited. She told me he was stretched out in her office, pale and listless. By the time I arrived he was perched on the edge of the cot, revived and talking about the tooth fairy.

"The tooth fairy brings me fifty dollars," he was telling the nurse. She looked startled. He often gets dollars confused with cents.

A plastic container in the shape of a tooth hung around his neck. He pried it open and showed me his tooth—small and jagged and pink with blood.

By this time, school was over. Spencer took me to his room to show me the class turtle and Sam Headley's chair. He took my hand and showed me the globe. There was a straight pin stuck in Indiana, just left of center.

"That's where we live," he said. "Next to the *d* in Indiana."

I took him home. That night at the dinner table he spoke of losing his tooth and how Mrs. Pizarek, the teacher's aide, took him to the rest room, then to the nurse's office. After supper, he drew a picture of Mrs. Pizarek holding his hand.

"That's my tooth," he said, pointing to a jagged tooth as large as his foot. My son hasn't yet learned about perspective. But then, neither have I.

*P*erspective: the capacity to view things in their true relations or relative importance.

I used to think the most important thing I could do was keep my children safe. That is a wild hope. Now I want for them to love, to trust, to believe. In God, in themselves, in others.

When we Quakers started planning our preschool, we had big dreams. We would start with preschool, then form a kindergarten and add one grade each year right up through high school. Our children would remain within our safe grasp. But it didn't work, and I am grateful. The embrace that starts with the wish to protect invariably becomes a love that suffocates.

We embrace our children, but there comes the time to step aside and let others love them, too. Mrs. Campbell, Mrs. Griffin, Mrs. Fruits, the school nurse, Mrs. Pizarek, and the incredible Sam Headley are waiting in the wings. They do not love our children as much as we do, but they love them in ways we cannot. It is not possible for us to give our children all the love they need. We can only give them so much, then must send them forth so that others might embrace them, too.

CHAPTER SIXTEEN

A Time to Refrain from Embracing

Things I Can't Abide

𝒯he older I get, the crankier I become, according to my wife. She believes in letting me know such things. If I am cranky, which is debatable, I come by it honestly. My father can be cranky. My grandfather tends toward crankiness and stories about my great-grandfather indicate he was cranky, too.

I told Joan I wasn't cranky, that I simply couldn't abide certain things and saw no reason to keep my feelings secret. After all, the author of Ecclesiastes reminds us, there is a time to refrain from embracing, which means that some things merit rejection. Therefore, as a matter of spiritual obedience, I am obligated to put my foot down about some things. I try not to be mean about it, but if I had my way I'd rid the world of certain annoyances.

One thing I can't abide is loud noise. Certain teenagers in our town drive pickup trucks with loud mufflers. They roar up and down our road. The racket bothers me to no end, even though I did the same thing when I was their age. I once drove an entire summer without any muffler on my car. I raced up and down the streets and revved my engine at the stoplights. It was the finest summer of my young life. Now that I'm older I don't like it and wish it were against the law. It wouldn't bother me at all to see a teenager or two arrested for driving a loud car.

This brings me to my second gripe: loud music in cars, the kind of music with lots of bass that you can hear thumping a mile away. Again, the problem here is young men who don't stop to think that other people might not want to hear their music. If you can call that music. I'm thinking of running for the town board on a platform of quiet streets. Any car playing loud music would be impounded and sold for scrap. Naturally, when I was a teenager I listened only to Bach and Lawrence Welk, and then only on headphones.

After noise and loud music in cars, the next thing I simply can't tolerate is barking dogs. I know it sounds un-American, but I'm not all that crazy about dogs to begin with. They stink, drool on your hand, and have bad breath; and after you pat their head your hands feel dirty. People who have dogs always assure me I will like their dog, and I always act as if I do even when I don't. I especially don't like dogs that bark night and day and I'm not inclined to think well of their owners, either. When I was growing up, I had a dog named Zipper who was the best dog in the world. Everyone who knew her agreed with me that she was exceptional.

Please bear in mind that in describing these annoyances, I'm not being cranky, but obedient. I'm merely living according to Ecclesiastes, which tells us there's a time to refrain from embracing certain things.

There are other things I don't like, things I think the world would be better off without. Yard work is one of them. I know people who enjoy yard work, but I don't and never have. The only time I'm grateful for yard work is when my wife wants me to go shopping with her and I tell her I would if I didn't have so much yard work. I could hire someone to do my yard work for me, but that isn't done in our town.

Another gripe I have is when people throw trash from their car windows. There's nothing worse than driving down the road behind someone who is throwing a fast-food bag in the ditch along the road. I wish I were a police officer and could pull them over, give them a ticket, and make them pick it up. If I were in charge, I would make people who litter spend the hottest day of the summer walking up and down the road picking up trash. The night before they had to do it, I'd dump a bunch of trash in the ditch just to make their job harder.

While I'm on the subject of cars again, another thing I don't like is when parents don't make their kids buckle their seat belts. People who don't strap their children in the car should be arrested, except for people like my parents who, in the eighteen years I lived with them, never had me wear a seat belt. But that was different.

Another of my pet peeves is climbing out of the bathtub and realizing I left my towel in the other bathroom. A couple times a year I stay in hotels, and despite all their faults, I'll say this about hotels: there are always plenty of towels in hotel bathrooms.

The absolute worst thing about traveling is, of course, flying on an airplane. If man has devised a more torturous way to travel, that way has escaped me. Cramped seats, long lines, bad food, and turbulence. Turbulence is a growing problem on air flights. During a recent flight, I peeked through my hands to see the beverage cart in midair and the stewardess hanging upside down from the luggage bin.

I hate it when I'm at the grocery store and hear people screaming at their children and swatting them. Dear Abby said the best thing to do when that happens is to go to the parents and gently offer to watch their children while they shop. I would do that, but I'm afraid they'd take me up on it and then I'd be stuck with the little monsters.

I will never embrace telephone solicitation. I still feel a slight thrill whenever the phone rings, thinking it might be someone calling with an incredible job offer or to tell me I won a grand prize. It never is. It's always someone trying to sell me something. If you're a telephone solicitor, don't waste your time. My house doesn't need new siding and I don't want to switch phone companies no matter how cheap it is.

$\mathcal{H}$ere are some other things I don't like and could never in good conscience embrace:

Politicians who do dumb, sneaky things, then blame other people.

My wife uses my tube of ChapStick sometimes. Then when I want to use it, it's red with her lipstick. Even though we smooch frequently, I don't like sharing my ChapStick.

I cannot abide a pastor who preaches longer than twenty minutes, unless, of course, it's me.

While we're on the subject of church, I don't like singing songs shown on the wall from an overhead projector. I like old songs sung from old hymnals.

I don't care for new houses, even though I live in one. The only thing that keeps me from buying an old house is that I hate working on old houses even more than I hate new houses.

I will never understand why some men don't raise the lid, then lower it when they're done.

I can't abide old acquaintances calling me on the phone under the guise of wanting to talk about old times, then end up asking me to have a party so they can sell detergent or paintings or baskets.

Those are the things that make me mad. If I were to think harder, I could probably come up with more. But I'm not going to, because I don't like to dwell on the negative. It goes against my personality. That's another thing I can't abide— negative people. I'm glad I'm not like that.

I have a confession. I often get mad at the wrong things. You probably didn't know this about me, but it's true. I complain about the dumbest things. World hunger scarcely fazes me, but if the man at McDonald's forgets to put ketchup on my hamburger, watch out. I'm not proud of this. A good start on wisdom is being able to judge which things merit anger and which things don't; which things we ought to embrace and which things we shouldn't.

I became a Christian after reading the Bible and discovering, much to my delight, that Jesus and I didn't care for many of the same things. He didn't like loud music either, which is why the apostles didn't bring their boom boxes along on their journeys. I'm not certain where he stood on long-lost friends who want you to throw a detergent party—the Bible doesn't say. Jesus also didn't like people to grouch about stuff that didn't matter. He called such people "gnat-strainers." I'm glad I'm not like that.

CHAPTER SEVENTEEN

A Time to Seek

A Quiet Satisfaction

One of life's finer pleasures is the feeling of superiority. By that I do not mean the ugly type of superiority when we suppose our race or nationality is better than another. I am speaking of the quiet satisfaction one feels after working hard to master a particular vocation, subject, or sport.

I am not very handy at fixing things, nor am I very organized. But my neighbor Joe is even less competent than I in these matters, which makes me feel superior. It is a wonderful feeling. In fairness to Joe, I must say he excels in all other matters. He is a wonderful man, a loving father and husband, can beat me in basketball, is treasured by his mother, and goes to church every week. But to my intense delight, he is thoroughly incompetent in matters of home repair and tool organization. He spends an inordinate amount of time looking for his tools. And when he finds them, he doesn't know what to do with them.

I have a Peg-Board panel in my garage where I hang my tool collection, which includes three wrenches, two hammers, a saw, six screwdrivers, and a spoke shaver my grandfather gave me in the event I ever need to build a wooden wagon wheel. I went to the hardware store and bought a pint of black paint and a small paintbrush and painted the outline of each tool on the Peg-Board. That way, when Joe comes and borrows a tool without asking, I can tell at a glance that he snuck in and took it.

Joe has a Peg-Board in his garage, too. He has five shovels and three mops hanging on it. Why a man needs five shovels and three mops is something Joe has never adequately explained. His hand tools are crammed in a cardboard box alongside his wheelbarrow. I suggested he rid himself of the mops and shovels and hang his hand tools on the Peg-Board. I proposed he paint outlines around his tools so he could tell at a glance if all his tools were present and accounted for. I even gave him my black paint and paintbrush to use, but he lost them before he could get the outlines painted.

*F*or some time, Joe has wanted to build a storage shed in his backyard even though they aren't allowed in our neighborhood. No detached buildings except for gazebos, the rules read. Since Joe can't build a storage shed, he wants to erect a gazebo and store his junk in there. This mystifies me. Joe has a four-car garage. If a man can't store his things in a four-car garage, he has too much stuff and needs to hold a sale. Joe says the problem is his wife, who brings things home quicker than he can organize them. Joe takes his problems like a man; he blames them on his wife.

Joe and I were trying to get his tractor started one Saturday and were looking for his battery charger. "It's around here somewhere," he said, nudging boxes aside with his foot. "I'll find it any minute now."

I had my doubts.

Then he said, "If they let me build a storage shed, I'd know where my battery charger was."

I had my doubts about that, too.

It was then I made up my mind that I was going to get Joe organized, even if it killed me.

Getting a man organized is no small task and should not be undertaken lightly or frivolously. It involves undoing a lifetime of bad habits. The person needing help must be willing to undergo a grueling process. Fortunately, Joe was at the end of his rope, admitted his need for a change, and was willing to endure the hard work necessary to become an organized man. "I'm tired of tripping over boxes and spending an hour looking for a flashlight," he told me. He wept as he confessed, a man broken by clutter.

"Could you help me?" he pleaded, a lone tear coursing down his cheek.

We started with his garage.

"You need shelves," I told him. "Lots of shelves." A man can never have too many shelves.

Joe didn't have any shelves. He did have a credenza his wife had brought home. No doubt useful for the office, but a space waster in a garage. "Get it out of here," I told Joe. "Give it away, sell it, burn it, throw it in a ditch somewhere, but get it out of here." I'm not ordinarily a bossy man, but when you undertake to organize a friend, you have to be firm.

I called Bill Eddy, who came the next Saturday and took the credenza to store his fishing equipment. It will soon occur to Bill that a credenza is a lousy place to store fishing equipment, but by then he'll be stuck with it. When you undertake to organize a man, morals and scruples can't stand in the way.

I estimated it would take seven hundred dollars to get Joe's garage fit for habitation, what with having to buy twelve shelves, three bicycle hangers, a workbench, a ten-foot stepladder, and a color television to watch Indiana University basketball. But first we had to convince his wife, which was an easy matter.

"It's cheaper than a gazebo," I told her.

We started on a Tuesday. Joe had a pile of junk heaped in the corner. I asked him what it was.

"Well, there's an orange couch in there somewhere," he said.

I don't wish to be immodest, but in addition to my strong organizational skills, I also possess a keen sense of style. I suggested Joe put the orange couch on his front porch, a step I consider to be the epitome of gracious living. Over the next two days, we hung twelve shelves, built a workbench, hung three bicycles, serviced his mower, put his tools on a Peg-Board panel, and outlined them with black paint. We stored the dog food, cat food, and birdseed in plastic bins, hung his weed whacker, mounted his electric screwdriver to the left of the workbench and his fire extinguisher to the right. The television is on the second shelf, eye level, and the lawn chairs hang beside the utility sink.

*I*t is now a fine garage, and whenever I see it I swell with pride, knowing I had a hand in it. Joe has cut his seeking time considerably. When he needs a wrench, he knows right where to find it. He takes undisguised pleasure in his newfound organization and is even becoming proficient at home repairs.

"Why didn't I do this sooner?" he asked me. "Now I know where everything is and don't have to storm around looking."

I told Joe he shouldn't despair his years spent seeking, that it made him appreciate his new organized state.

Seeking teaches us things finding never can.

Back when I was a pastor, people would often comment to me how they wished they'd come upon God sooner. I would point out the blessings of a faith not easily found, how a faith found too quickly isn't generally a faith worth holding. Scott Wagoner, a pastor friend of mine, cautions his flock never to despise their search for the sacred, that regret dishonors that holy process. Instead of despairing our times of seeking without finding, we should remember that seeking makes the finding all the sweeter. So whether we're looking for a wrench or looking for God, we ought not despise the seeking.

When my wife complained about not being able to find her car keys, I explained that seeking was not to be despised.

Joan thought about that for a while, then asked, "Why did I have to marry a theologian?"

"Because you couldn't find anyone better," I told her.

"Maybe I just didn't look long enough," she replied.

She may have a point.

CHAPTER EIGHTEEN

A Time to Lose

The Royal Theater

One Saturday evening my wife and I walked the mile into town to see a movie.

Every Saturday night since 1927, the bright lights of the Royal Theater marquee have spilled across Washington Street and onto the courthouse lawn. But that Saturday night the rows of bulbs were lifeless and the doors locked. A piece of paper taped to the door bore the sad message: Closed.

Three thousand six hundred and ninety-two movies killed off by a paper on the door. Charlie Chaplin in *The Little Dictator*, Claudette Colbert with *It Happened One Night*, Humphrey Bogart and Katharine Hepburn in *The African*

Queen, Bob and Bing in the road movies, Jimmy Stewart with *It's a Wonderful Life* and *Mr. Smith Goes to Washington,* John Wayne as Rooster Cogburn and Harrison Ford as Indiana Jones. Never to return. Gone. That's what came to mind when I read that sad, defeated word. *Closed.*

My first memory of the Royal Theater was when I was seven and my parents took us to see *Chitty Chitty Bang Bang* starring Dick Van Dyke as Caractacus Potts. Five kids at a quarter each, plus two adults at fifty cents apiece. Total bill: two dollars and twenty-five cents. It was a splendid evening and such a fine memory that it was all I could do to not name my first son Caractacus.

Robert and Sophie Ahart and their four daughters ran the Royal Theater. Mr. Ahart wore a suit and tie, sold tickets, and maintained order. Mrs. Ahart and her smiling daughters sold popcorn and candy. Popcorn was a dime, candy a nickel. Jimmy Anderson was the projectionist, janitor, and usher. He would climb the ladder to the projection booth, load the reels, fire up the projector, and observe the moviegoers through a little window. You couldn't see him, but you could sense him perched there, overseeing you.

*T*he Royal Theater had two rules: no talking and no resting your feet on the seat in front of you. When people started talking, Jimmy stopped the movie until it got quiet. He kept an eye peeled for people who rested their feet on the seats in front of them. If he saw a violation, he would climb down from the projection booth, walk up beside the offender, and crack him on the kneecap with a flashlight. He did this with young and old; it made no difference.

While you were lying on the floor, clutching your knee and weeping, Jimmy would clarify the rule. Get your feet off the chair or you'll have to leave. Then he'd climb back up the ladder to the projection booth. To this day, there are people in our town who walk with a hobble. Other than that it was a warmly hospitable place, and from 1968 to 1977, I spent every Saturday night there on the right-hand side, third row from the back, aisle seat.

I saw my first, and only, horror movie at the Royal Theater. *Frogs,* starring Ray Milland. Vacationers on an island resort were overwhelmed and eaten by frogs. We had a farm pond in our back field. I went home that night and listened to the frogs croak and didn't sleep a wink. Not that night or the two nights that followed. I've never seen another horror movie. Being the parent of small children is scary enough.

I was not at the Royal Theater when *King Kong* was shown. I wish I had been. Mr. Ahart hired a man to dress up as a gorilla. Halfway through the movie, when King Kong was ready to snatch Fay Wray, Mr. Ahart turned off the lights, stopped the movie, and had the gorilla man run through the theater, grabbing people. The theater seated 450 people. Two hundred and twenty-five of them cleared out in under a minute.

When my wife and I were casting about for a house to buy, one of the criteria was to be within walking distance of the Royal Theater and other downtown charms. We spread a map of the town on the kitchen table, stuck the compass point on the Royal Theater, and drew a one-mile radius. Any house within the circle was fair game. With the theater gone, I feel less bound to this place and am considering a move to the country. Because we had the Royal Theater we never felt the need to own a television or video machine. Now with the theater gone, our whole lifestyle needs adjusting. We may have to buy a television.

The Royal passed slowly, like an old woman

succumbing to strokes. In 1947, the Central
Normal Teachers College shut down. The students comprised the bulk of the theater's
business and their departure did not bode well
for the Royal. In the 1950s, television came
along. I can't imagine why people preferred to sit
at home watching television when they could
have sat at the Royal Theater eating popcorn.
Even with Jimmy Anderson cracking your
kneecap, it was still a superior place and why the
townspeople didn't flock there is beyond me. In
the 1960s the Royal went from showing movies
every night to just four times a week. Then some
conglomerate built an eight-screen theater in the
next town over; that sealed the Royal's fate,
though it took some time to realize it.

I want to blame someone for her passing, to
point my finger at one person and charge
him with her death. Of course, there's no such a
person. It's all of us. It's the video store that came
to town and popcorn you can pop in your
microwave and cable television and four-lane
highways that whisk you into the city for dinner
and a movie. It's Hollywood, who stopped making the Lone Ranger and Green Hornet serials

that used to bring in the kids. It's Movietone News, who stopped making newsreels when folks turned to Walter Cronkite for their news.

What saddens me most about the Royal's death is that now there is one less thing my sons can do that I did as a matter of routine at their age. I used to build campfires in the woods across from my home. Now it's a town park and campfires aren't permitted. I used to ride my bike to the hardware store and look at the pocket-knives in the glass case. Now the old hardware store is closed and the new one is out on the highway, and they don't sell pocketknives. I used to eat sundaes at Lawrence's Drugstore, but it's vanished, too. The Royal Theater was my last great hope, and now it is lost to us and I'm desolate beyond all reason.

More than a theater died. The newspaper from the city carried an article about it. *Local Business Closes,* the headline read. That is a huge understatement. The Royal Theater was so much more than a local business. It was a place of wonder, of romance, of drama and dreams. Gorillas roamed her aisles. Kneecaps were bruised for life. Romances were launched in her sacred seats. The Royal Theater was a shrine to all that's good and decent in America. Now my sons won't know its pleasures, and that grieves me. Watching Roy Rogers at the Royal Theater provided my moral foundation. I learned to open the door for ladies, to never shoot a man in the back, to take my hat off inside, and to revere my mother. I was taught that my word was my bond, that there are good guys and bad guys and that bad guys always lost, so be good. The Ten Commandments couldn't have taught it plainer.

The lights outside the Royal Theater are now dark, the ticket booth empty. Display cases, once graced with colorful movie posters, are now vacant and forlorn. But I remember when it was not so. And when I stood before the Royal with my wife on that recent Saturday evening, I remembered back to 1968. It was the last year they showed Western matinees. The film was crackly; the sound popped with age. Gene Autry was sitting astride Champion, singing "Back in the Saddle Again." Back when a friend was a friend.

I've just lost a friend. This story has no moral, no counsel on living well. It's just that one of my friends died, and I felt the need to tell you a little something about her.

Chapter Nineteen

A Time to Keep

The Old Cigar Box

As a Quaker, I am compelled to embrace certain virtues I would not otherwise find attractive. Since Quakers are pacifists, I can't fight with anyone. By and large, this has not been a problem, except once when I had a mean boss and wanted to punch him in the nose but couldn't because I was a Quaker. Instead I quit and found a new job. But there for a while, I wished I were a Baptist.

In addition to pacifism, Quakers are sticklers for honesty. If you ever buy a used car, buy one from a Quaker. If you ask, we'll tell you everything that's wrong with the car and whether it's been wrecked. But you have to ask, because we won't volunteer the information. We're honest but not stupid.

Quakers value equality. We believe women are equal to men and, if given the opportunity, can make just as big a mess of things as men can. We don't discriminate against people of color or folks who hold different views about God. We get along well with Muslims, Jews, and Buddhists but have been known to bicker with one another. In 350 years, we've had three major splits and numerous small fractures. It's a good thing we're pacifists, or blood would have been shed.

Peace, honesty, and equality are just some of the Quaker testimonies. We also have a high regard for simplicity and have written books about it, some of them hundreds of pages thick. We believe clothing should be practical and not flashy, the same as our cars, and that our food should be nourishing and plain. When we eat in fancy restaurants, we feel guilty. The big difference between denominations isn't theology but the things that make us feel guilty.

Regarding simplicity, Quakers believe when you open a closet door, nothing should fall out. We visit one another and when our hosts have left the room, we open the closets to see if they pass the simplicity test. We also believe if you have to cram your sweaters in the dresser drawer, if you have to push them down as you close the drawer, you have too many sweaters and should give some away. Episcopalians believe you should buy a bigger dresser.

I am a good Quaker when it comes to pacifism. I've never killed anyone and don't intend to. I do okay with honesty. Every now and then I tell a lie, mostly to my wife in response to questions like "Would you mind doing the dishes?" or "Do you like this dress?"

I try always to be honest in my business dealings and don't do business with people who aren't. In case you are reading this and happen to work for the Internal Revenue Service, I am scrupulously honest on my taxes and every year pay more than I owe. You can trust me on that, since I'm an honest Quaker.

The one Quaker test I can't pass is simplicity. I dress simply. When I eat in a fancy restaurant, I feel guilty. I give my sweaters away. But when it comes to the closet test, I'm a miserable failure. This is because I'm a sentimentalist and am unable to part with anything that holds even a sliver of meaning for me. I have an old cigar box in my bedroom closet, up on the top shelf. It's full to the brim with an assortment of things that are worthless to everyone but me. There's a piece of paper with a poem written on it. When I was sixteen, a girl named Nora gave it to me. It is a beautiful poem, lyrical and sweet, though a bit steamy. It talks about forming as one and wanting to love me if I'll come close enough to let her. Heady stuff for a sixteen-year-old boy. It's the only poem a girl ever wrote me so I'm keeping it. I showed it to my wife, then asked her to write me a poem. Joan wrote,

> *Roses are red,*
> *Violets are blue.*
> *How can I write poetry*
> *And watch your children, too?*

I've also kept the receipt from the first new bicycle I ever owned. I bought it on June 16, 1975. I was fourteen years old. The bike was a green Schwinn Varsity. It had ten speeds, eight of which I never used. Serial number DL545900. It cost $138.78, which included tax and a bicycle lock. When I bought it, my parents said they'd pay me back, but they never did. Lyn Larison

down at the bank says at a modest 7 percent
interest rate compounded annually my parents
owe me $691.18. I called to tell them and they
laughed at me. I'm thinking of retaining legal
counsel.

I keep a little money in my cigar box. Not
much, just a little. A 1953 two-dollar bill to be
precise, given to me by my father. I guess this
means they only owe me $689.18. Do you
know which U.S. president appears on the two-
dollar bill? Thomas Jefferson. Thomas Jefferson
was our third president and a fine one. He also
wrote the Declaration of Independence in 1776.
We showed our appreciation by putting his picture on the two-dollar bill, a contemptible
denomination. I think we should promote
Thomas Jefferson to the fifty-dollar bill and
bump Grant down to the two-dollar bill. Grant
was a great general but a lousy president. He
didn't like Quakers, either.

At the bottom of my cigar box is the funeral
card from when my best friend, Tim Hadley, died
on May 25, 1981. I also kept the funeral card
from when his mother, Evelyn, died of cancer
twelve years later. My Grandma Norma passed
away on August 27, 1994. I have her funeral card,
too. The Christmas before my friend Tim died, he

gave me a list of things he wanted for Christmas.
I keep the list in my cigar box. In 1980, Tim
wanted an eight-track tape, a flannel shirt, or a
set of socket wrenches. He also wrote down that
he wanted long underwear but then crossed it
out. When Tim died he was still young enough
not to want underwear for Christmas.

My wife doesn't have a cigar box and
looks askance at me whenever I pull
mine down to rummage through it. She isn't
sentimental, except when it comes to our sons.
Then she saves everything. When our little boy
Sam is forty years old with children of his own,
we'll be able to remember that my wife first had
labor pains at 1 A.M. on February 24, 1995, and
that Sam was born eight hours later at 9:09 A.M.
We'll remember that because Joan wrote it down
in the journal she keeps in her nightstand. Once
a week, ever since our kids were born, she's written something about them. When Spencer was
three years old, he dressed as a spotted leopard
for Halloween. My wife sewed the outfit herself.
It's all there in the journal.

Most mothers are keepers. When I was seven
years old, I bought my mother a plastic canary

at Danners' Five-and-Dime. She hung it on the curtain rod over the kitchen sink where it's been ever since. She's had the kitchen remodeled twice since then, but that green-and-yellow canary still perches on the curtain rod and sings its silent song. That's a mother for you.

When Jesus was alive, his mother didn't keep a journal. Whenever he did anything special, she committed it to memory. Luke says she kept all these things in her heart. That's a good place to keep things, in your heart. Close at hand, just like that canary on the curtain rod.

There are things my sons have done I thought would be branded in my memory, but time assailed and they are gone. I could not keep them in my heart. I wish I had written them down and put them in my cigar box. It's a wise person who knows what to keep and what to cast away. I keep bicycle receipts from 1975. My wife keeps journals and memories sweet and tender. It's best to keep things in your heart, but if you can't, cigar boxes and journals run a close second.

CHAPTER TWENTY

A Time to Cast Away

Jubilee

My wife and I have moved four times in fourteen years, once every three and a half years. The average American family packs up and moves every five years. We're above-average movers. During the same time period, my brother David moved twelve times, while my mother-in-law, Ruby Apple, has lived in the same farmhouse on Grimes Lake Road since September 15, 1940.

I'm not proud that we've moved so much. I tend to be suspicious of people who move a lot. I wonder what they're running from. Are they moving because they owe money? Sometimes people move because they've switched jobs. Why can't they hold a job? I don't think I'd hire some-one who moved every three and a half years.

The first time we moved was when we got married. That's normal for newlyweds, so I'm not ashamed of that move at all. The second time we moved was because the house we were living in was going to be torn down, so that move wasn't our fault, either. The third time we moved was when I accepted a call to pastor a church in the city. That was the Lord's doing, so I had no choice. The fourth time we moved was to simplify our lives, which is an admirable goal. Did you notice that when other people move it's because of moral failures, but when I move it's for good reasons?

While I am suspicious of people who move a lot, moving does have its benefits. If we live in one place long enough, we pile up a lot of stuff. Moving forces us to cast away the old clothes and unused Christmas gifts which would other-wise fill our closets. Packing our belongings compels us to decide whether we value some-thing enough to move it. If we never move, we can shove it in the closet and forget about it. When my parents die, I will cry for two rea-sons—because I'm sad and because they haven't moved in thirty years and their closets are full.

So are their basement, attic, and barn. I hope they move before they die.

*J*oan enjoys moving, mostly because she likes throwing things away. Every spring she plunders our house, room by room, closet by closet. She seizes every item—every article of clothing, every knickknack, every book, every toy, every small appliance—lifts it in the air and asks, "Has this been used in the past year?" She eyes me as I answer—a living, breathing lie detector. If I tell her I haven't used it, she hurls it in a box and hauls it to the Salvation Army. If she thinks I'm lying, she hurls it in the box just the same. I now write on things when I've last used them. If you look closely at the right cuff of my blue dress shirt, you can make out the words *last worn April 14.*

I know a lady who never throws anything away. She has four couches in her living room because when she buys a new couch, she can't bear to discard the old one. Couches line her walls—five in all. Four in her living room and one in her kitchen, pulled up to the table. You sit at the couch and eat, your plate at eye level. Couches aren't her only collectibles. She saves newspapers, magazines, soup labels, and coffee cans. In her closet is a box labeled *String Too Short to Use*. My wife went to visit her and broke out with hives.

My first bicycle was handed down from my brothers. When I outgrew it, it was worn out, so I pushed it to the dump and left it there. Within two weeks it was returned to me three times by people who thought it was a sin to throw something away. I grew up on the road to the dump. On Saturday mornings I'd watch townspeople drive to the dump, their trucks filled with debris. Two hours later they'd return, headed toward home, their trucks piled even higher.

I wonder if our willingness to cast things away is a measure of our spiritual well-being. Consider this: the first thing the followers of Jesus did was leave their stuff behind. Jesus said to Peter and Andrew, "Follow me," and immediately they left their nets and followed him. Peter and Andrew were not from around here. Otherwise, they'd have had a garage sale first.

The same is true of James and John. They left their boat and their father to follow Jesus. He also asked the rich young ruler to leave his stuff behind, which the young man couldn't bring himself to do. He loved his things too much and went away sad. From what I can tell, it's the only time anyone ever went away from Jesus sad. I try to remember that whenever I think things will make me happy.

Though Peter gave up his possessions to follow Jesus, he had some misgivings about it. After the young ruler went away sad, Peter raised the subject with Jesus:

"We've left everything to follow you. What will we get?"

The first time I read that, I thought Jesus would lower the boom on Peter. But he didn't. I suspect Jesus understood the fear Peter had in letting go of things, how the nets Peter left behind promised a comforting security. Jesus understood the seduction of possessions, but knew our belongings offer a false security, which is why he challenged his followers to put their trust in God alone. "If God so clothes the grass of the field," he said, "how much more will he clothe you?... Seek first God's kingdom, and all these things shall be yours as well.... Do not be anxious about anything...."

For centuries, Christians extolled the riches of simplicity. We started out to do good but settled for doing well. A poor trade. Now I fear we are losing our way with our luxury cars and custom homes and bloated retirement funds. We ask the Lord for our daily bread, then sit down to steak. Our barns and bellies are full. But Jesus taught that the day our barns are full is the day of our downfall.

Trusting in things has always been a problem for God's people. The Israelites dealt with it by holding a year of Jubilee. The year of Jubilee is described in the book of Leviticus, chapter 25, right after the eye-for-an-eye and tooth-for-a-tooth stuff. We liked that part so much, we stopped reading and have been blind and toothless ever since. We should have kept reading to learn about Jubilee.

Jubilee was God's way of taming our lust for things. Every fiftieth year, all lands reverted back to their original owners. If you owned any slaves, you set them free. It was one of the less popular religious traditions and wasn't observed with much diligence. In fact, some scholars say it was never observed, except once when the Israelites had made God mad and were looking to get back on his good side. After a while they dropped Jubilee altogether. Today we celebrate Christmas, which has gone a long way toward curbing our materialism.

Knew a man growing up named Harley Jacobs. Harley was a keeper, never threw anything away. In a neighborhood of serene people, Harley was an oddity, a man frantic with acquisition and on a constant quest for more. After Harley died, his son poked through his house, stacked and piled with forty years of buying, and decided not to get involved. He shut off the water, turned down the furnace, unplugged the toaster, and locked her tight. He is a religious man, so every Sunday morning he prays a tornado will swoop through town and carry his father's house away. His prayers are to no avail— the house still stands, full to the brim.

Since I move every three and a half years, my sons won't have that problem with me. I like to tell myself that my ability to let go of things is due to my spiritual maturity, but the truth is that I can't stand clutter. While I can surrender my possessions, I find it hard to cast off my fears. I lie awake at night and worry about the mortgage payment and what will happen to me when I'm old. I used to stay awake because my children were afraid and needed comfort. Now they are older and much braver, and I am older and so much more afraid. I long for a new Jubilee, that I might cast my fears away.

CHAPTER TWENTY-ONE

A Time to Rend

Pretenders

When we moved into our new house, I subscribed to *CountryLife* magazine. I had bought the magazine at the grocery store because there was a house on the cover that had something in common with our new home. It had doors and windows and was painted red. There was a subscription form in the magazine offering a *68% Discount!* over the newsstand price.

"Look at all the money we can save," I told my wife, and filled out the form.

A few weeks later, Claudia from *CountryLife* wrote us a letter. She was very gracious. She said she was glad we were joining the *CountryLife* family and was certain we'd end up good friends since we had so much in common. Claudia (we were already on a first-name basis) congratulated us for saving all this money by subscribing when we did. She misspelled my name, but what's a little mistake among friends?

The first issue arrived just as we were getting ready to put down new vinyl flooring in our kitchen. A picture in the magazine showed a kitchen with wood floors.

"Would you look at that," I told Joan. "Isn't that beautiful?"

She agreed that it was nice but that it was too expensive and we couldn't afford it. I reminded her of all the money we had saved by subscribing to the magazine when we did. So for a mere two thousand dollars more, we had the floor people install wood floors.

"You did this just in time," the floor man told us. "Our prices go up next week. You've saved a lot of money." The magazine was paying for itself already.

The next edition of *CountryLife* had a grandfather clock in it. A few days later, I was walking past a store and there was one just like it in the window. A beautiful clock, handmade. I decided to buy it for my wife as a present. The man who made it delivered it to our house.

He set it up in our kitchen, next to the back door.

"You've bought a wonderful clock," he told us.

I asked him if it had a warranty.

"It's guaranteed for a lifetime," he said. "Unfortunately, it's for *my* lifetime and I'm eighty-one."

After the man left, Joan asked me why I bought her a clock. "I got the idea from *Country Life*," I told her. "Aren't you glad we subscribed?"

Over the next year, inspired by the magazine, I bought two cupboards, three lamps, eight chairs, a chandelier, two pictures, a quilt, a porch swing, and a table. I never would have thought of these things if not for *CountryLife*. Instead, I would have wasted our money on dumb things like college funds and IRAs.

We had signed up for only one year. After eight months, Claudia wrote from the magazine to tell us how much she'd enjoyed our friendship over the past year and hoped we'd be renewing for another year. Then she let us in on a little secret. Because we were her friends, if we signed up for two years we'd enjoy a *72% Discount!* over the newsstand price. What a deal! I showed Claudia's letter to my wife, who plucked it from my hand and threw it in the wastebasket.

"That magazine is going to break us," Joan said.

I wrote Claudia to tell her we wouldn't be renewing our subscription, that we couldn't afford it.

The next month Claudia wrote again, saying she couldn't believe she hadn't heard from us. Apparently she didn't get my letter, so I wrote her again and told her once more that we didn't want to renew, though we wanted to remain friends. I included our phone number and a map to our house so she could visit us sometime. I wanted to show her there were no hard feelings.

Claudia wrote again. She said that losing me was a bit like losing a friend. She was disappointed. She thought I enjoyed our friendship. In fact, Claudia and all the other folks at the magazine met to talk about my not renewing my subscription and wanted to offer me a free gift! Claudia said they had worked for months to pick out just the right gift for me.

I felt terrible about this. I think I hurt her feelings. I wrote back to tell her she didn't need to send me a free gift, that I wasn't upset with her and that we could still be friends. Besides, if Claudia sends me a present, then I'll have to send her one and I can't afford it right now.

Truthfully, I'm a little worried about Claudia and hope she doesn't go off the deep end. In retrospect, I sense she took our friendship more seriously than I did. I hope she doesn't do something drastic. I encouraged her to become active in a church or club where she could meet new friends. I told her she had her whole life ahead of her, that today was the first day of the rest of her life. I hope it helps.

I don't mean to cast aspersions, but these magazine people are so sensitive. I had the same problem with Harold from *Newsweek*. We were friends for five years; then I stopped taking the magazine and he hasn't spoken to me since.

I don't understand this, how people can be friends and then break it off. I have four friends, who've been my friends for years. I would have more friends, but I don't have the time. It takes time to be a friend. I've always suspected that my friends are better friends to me than I am to them. But they are my friends. I should never have agreed to be Claudia's friend. She wanted more from me than I was able to give. Now her feelings are hurt and there's no telling where it will end.

To be truthful, I'm a little disappointed in Claudia and Harold. I expect a lot from my friends, like loyalty. I try to repay them in kind. If we have problems, we work them out. We don't bribe one another with presents, nor do we put each other on guilt trips. What were Claudia and Harold thinking?

The word *friend* has been watered down. If we spend five minutes with someone, we're suddenly "friends." I suspect people are wanting to be nice, which is fine, but it has the effect of cheapening our more enduring friendships. Today, "friends" are people we used to call acquaintances; "good friends" are people we like; "old friends" are people we've known a long time; and "dear friends" are the people we used to call "friends" back when the word meant something.

This cheapening of our language is because big corporations, like the corporation that owns

CountryLife, use these hallowed words like cheap trinkets. We're no longer their customers, which is such a cold, impersonal term. We're their friends! I've always wanted to be friends with a corporation, haven't you?

"Set the table and bring out the good china, honey, our friends from the BigBucks Corporation are here!"

It is time to rend. I'm closing the door on Claudia, who probably isn't a real person anyway. If I were to call and ask for Claudia, the operator would transfer me to the subscriptions department where all the women use the name Claudia, which is the code word for the subscriptions department. One hundred women wearing headphones, perched at computer terminals, saying, "Hello, my name is Claudia. How may I help you?" I wonder *which* Claudia was my friend?

The author of Proverbs reminds us, "There are friends who pretend to be friends, but there is a friend who is closer than a brother." I have a feeling Claudia and Harold were pretenders.

I have four friends who'd walk through fire for me. When I lie down at night and count my blessings, they come to mind, right after my family and just before my comfortable home, which, like the house on the magazine cover, has doors and windows and is painted red.

CHAPTER TWENTY-TWO

A Time to Sew

A Joining Together

$\mathcal{M}$y wife and I began our courtship with a disagreement.

I maintain that our first date was on June 9, 1982, when we went for a bicycle ride through the country to the Sugar Grove Friends Cemetery. Joan insists our first date was the next month, when we ate dinner at a revolving restaurant in the city. We dined through five revolutions. By the third revolution, I was delirious with love. On the fourth revolution I asked her to marry me. On the fifth revolution she declined, saying she never accepted offers of matrimony on a first date.

I pointed out that it wasn't our first date, it

was our second. She said visiting a cemetery was not a date; I maintained it was. We've lived with this disagreement ever since. Despite this contentious start, we've enjoyed a relatively cordial marriage. When our sons ask how we met, I tell them their mother was walking the streets. She was out for an evening walk; I spied her from my window and raced outside to introduce myself. There were many people who walked past my home, and I never raced out to meet any of them. But when I saw Joan, I dispensed with tradition and made her acquaintance. The next day, June 9, when she walked by again, I invited her to ride bicycles out to the Quaker cemetery, which she agreed to do, thus making it our first date.

She was a college student, away from home, working to earn money. She rented a bedroom and hot plate at Mary Wimsett's house. It was the summer of Mary's slow and fading death. Joan would lie awake through the night listening for her death rattle. In the evenings, I would take Joan on bicycle rides to local cemeteries. It was a morbid summer and when it came time for her to return to classes, she was secretly relieved.

*W*hen we first met, Joan had a boyfriend, which was not a hindrance to me since I knew our love was destined. "We could sooner stop the tides," I told her. Nevertheless, Joan took her boyfriend home to meet her mother, an ominous development. The morning she left I climbed on my bicycle and pedaled the hundred miles to her hometown. When I arrived, I phoned her mother's house to let Joan know that by an odd coincidence I happened to be in town on a bicycle trip and did she want to join me for supper.

She invited me to supper at her mother's, who served fried chicken and appeared slightly confused the entire evening. But I was not confused. Indeed, my mind was never clearer. The boyfriend must go. I took him aside and declared my intentions, then climbed back on my bike and pedaled home, dreaming of Joan the entire way.

I planted myself on Mary Wimsett's front porch to await Joan's return. "There's going to be a wedding," I told Mrs. Wimsett. She sat beside me, recalling her courtship with her husband, H. O. Wimsett. The widow Wimsett was clearly on my side and pledged, in her few remaining days, to assist me.

When Joan and her boyfriend drove up the driveway, Mary Wimsett advised, "Mind your manners and go open her car door. Ladies like manners." I hurried to open Joan's door. It was a stirring moment for me. I recall it now in slow motion. Sweeping to her side and holding the door open. Taking her slender hand and assisting her out. Oh, the thrill of touching that wondrous hand. I tingled to my spine. After seventeen years, that thrill has not diminished. Her boyfriend crumpled in the face of my zeal, climbed back in his car, and was never heard from again.

The next weekend, I took Joan to dinner at the revolving restaurant, where I proposed and she declined. I proposed once a week for the next year, and after a proper time she accepted. We were joined at the Quaker meetinghouse in Paoli, Indiana. When it came time to repeat the vows, I was so overcome I could barely speak them. During the prayer of blessing, I could hear weeping behind me. It was my father, similarly stricken. We are a passionate people.

Whenever I perform a wedding, I read the same vows I pledged the day I was married. "In the presence of the Lord, and before these friends, I take thee to be my wife, promising, with divine assistance, to be unto thee a loving and faithful husband, as long as we both shall live." I never make it through those vows without my voice catching.

I officiate at a handful of weddings every year, but no more than that because I don't enjoy it. I stopped enjoying weddings when they became an industry. When weddings were a religious celebration to affirm God's blessings, I enjoyed them. When they became a fashion show costing more than a car, they lost their appeal. If an engaged couple wants me to marry them and all they talk about are the colors and the string quartet, I want no part of it.

As long as we're on the subject, I want to mention that I don't put much stock in premarital counseling, either. This goes against the usual practice, which is to batter the prospective couple with a myriad of psychological tests. The best way to tell if a marriage will make it is to see if the man opens the door for the woman. If he doesn't, then he won't be inclined to extend larger considerations and the marriage is bound to fail. Any man who won't open the door for his wife will also neglect to lower the toilet seat, which we all know is the chief cause of divorce. The psychological tests don't tell you if the man is going to leave the toilet seat up. Instead, their purpose is to see whether the prospective couple have anything in common. Experts believe common interests are the secret of a successful marriage. Well, Joan and I have little in common, except for this—we are each unswervingly devoted to the person we married.

Our premarital test warned against our joining. It pointed out the likely area of conflict—arguments about money. Mostly because we didn't have any. So we came up with a plan about how to spend whatever money was left after taxes. We gave 10 percent to the church. We saved 10 percent. And the remaining five dollars, we lived on.

The tragedy the test predicted never arose. Our lack of resources didn't cause us to bicker, it challenged us to work as a team. It caused us to learn the difference between wants and needs and how to find happiness in one another instead of in things. I hear this has happened with millions of other couples, something the people who devised the test never considered. That's why I don't have much faith in tests, and why I still watch to see if the man opens the door for the lady.

We give the tests to convince ourselves that we're doing something to stem the hemorrhage of divorce. But most studies indicate that pre-marital tests and counseling offer only a marginal benefit, if any at all. The best predictor of our marital happiness is our parents' marriage. If they were in love, the chances are good that we will be, too. If they weren't, our chances for marital happiness are diminished. I don't have a study backing me up; this is just my hunch.

One Sunday afternoon when our children were little, I got mad at my wife and left home. I was gone for only twenty minutes, but in that twenty minutes both of my sons asked if I would ever come home. If I could ever undo a moment, it would be that one. Now I'm worried that my sons will think storming off is the best way to solve your problems. So I have some work to do.

The sewing together of two people is never-ending. Marriage is a quilt that always lies unfinished. Too many of us assume the work is finished when we say "I do." I thought that, too, but quickly learned otherwise.

The meal at the revolving restaurant cost $24.13. I saved the receipt in my cigar box. When I pulled out my wallet to pay the check, I fancied myself a man of wealth. To this day I remember that feeling.

Now I'm learning where my treasure is, and it isn't in my wallet.

CHAPTER TWENTY-THREE

A Time to Keep Silence

On Good Shoes,
Old Friends, and Silence

The older I get, the more I appreciate three things. Comfortable shoes are one. Old friends are another. And the third is silence.

There are other things I appreciate, but good shoes, old friends, and silence strike me as basic ingredients of a quality life. I've always worn good shoes, even when I didn't earn a lot of money. This was because my mother taught me never to skimp on anything that came between me and the ground. Whenever I purchase shoes or car tires, I don't pinch pennies.

My friend Jim is a wise man, except when it comes to shoes. He used to brag about how inexpensive his shoes were. Because he wore cheap shoes, he now has bad feet and can barely walk when he gets up in the morning. Jim doesn't brag about his cheap shoes anymore. Even if he started wearing good shoes, it probably wouldn't help. Once your feet are ruined, that's it.

I have good feet because for the past twenty years I've worn L. L. Bean ankle-high leather chukkas, built on a Dublin last. Size 9. I buy a new pair every three years. They are expensive shoes and worth every penny. I keep several new pairs in my closet just in case L. L. Bean stops making them. If I were ranking the characteristics of a blessed life, good shoes would be near the top.

Along with comfortable shoes, I would list old friends. By old friends I don't mean friends I've known a long time. I mean people it seems I've known forever. How long you've known someone is no indication of your fondness for them. An old friend is someone I no longer feel the need to impress. I have lots of regular friends, but only four old friends. I'm not going to name their names, because I don't want to hurt the feelings of the people who are just regular friends.

The third quality of the blessed life is silence. The older I get the more I crave it. People in my family start losing their hearing around the age of seventy. What a wonderful coincidence that we start losing our hearing the same time we start appreciating silence. By the time you're seventy, you've heard the best sounds this world has to offer—your grandchildren, Hank Williams, and katydids in August. By silence I don't mean an atmosphere void of any sound. I mean an atmosphere free of radios, voices, engines, sirens, and television. Natural noises are fine. If I'm sitting on our porch swing and all I can hear are katydids, crickets, and frogs, I consider that silence. Wondrous silence. But if the teenage boy next door revs his car engine, it's no longer silent. It's the silence of katydids, crickets, and frogs that I crave.

I grew up Catholic but became a Quaker at the age of sixteen because the Quaker girls were prettier than the Catholic girls. Plus, the Quakers sang with more gusto. The only thing I didn't like about the Quakers was the silence. The pastor would offer a brief message. Then those Quakers would sit in their quiet rows, standing every now and then to offer a word from the

Lord. Being sixteen years old, I found it tedious and boring, but I stuck with it due to the girls. Now I am an elder in that same Quaker meeting. The pastor offers a brief message and we sit there in our quiet rows, enveloped in holy silence. It is never long enough. Five minutes pass. The teenagers squirm and pass notes, but I relish the peace. On the Sundays I preach, I stretch out the silence before nodding to Mike Neely to begin the singing. There is never enough silence to suit me. I could take entire days of it.

I have friends who can name the very day of their Christian conversion. I am that way about silence. I became an appreciator of peace and quiet on July 24, 1992, the day our first child was born. This is nothing against my son, whom I love deeply. I am simply acknowledging that there are trade-offs in life. You can either have peace and quiet or you can have children. You can't have both. I chose children and would choose them again. But I miss silence.

Because I can't have silence at home, I want it at church. There are basically two types of Quaker meetings. There are meetings that hire pastors and listen to them, and there are meetings that don't hire pastors and listen to God.

You can probably tell which type of Quaker meeting I prefer. The Quaker meeting I attend has the best of both worlds. We have a pastor. He listens to God and we listen to him. But I wish that, just once a month, we could sit in silence and hear it straight from God.

I begin every morning with silence by taking a walk in the woods and meadows next to my house. It's good exercise and I do it every day, unless it's raining or I've overslept and run out of time. But I hike those trails at least once a week. Actually, I haven't started yet, but I've been planning to start for quite some time now and am going to do it just as soon as I can find the right kind of hiking socks to wear with my L. L. Bean chukkas. You can ruin your feet if you don't wear the right socks.

People who have hiked those meadows and woods talk with me about it. They emerge from the trail at the side of my home and spy me on my porch swing. I offer them a glass of iced tea and we sit and visit. They describe the creek and the prairie meadow and the silence. They expect the creek and prairie meadow; the silence comes as a surprise. But there it is, waiting to greet them. No car noise, no radios, no sirens. Just the music of water over rocks and the song of bluebirds. It's enough to make me find those socks and get started.

*T*here lives a man down the road who hikes the trails every morning. It is the silence that draws him. He retired from a large corporation, having tired of hearing people drone on about their money and their success. He bore such noise for thirty years, then moved here for the peace and quiet. When he arrived he was jangled and nervous; now he is serene and composed. He attributes his healing to the silence, and I believe him.

One morning when we were visiting on my porch, I offered him a bit of wisdom from the Quaker William Penn: "True silence is rest for the mind. It is to the spirit what sleep is to the body—nourishment and refreshment." The retired man said he wished someone had read that to him when he was twenty years old. I told him it wouldn't have mattered, that silence is something you must grow to cherish—like comfortable shoes.

Most people claim to like silence, though I doubt it. If people wanted silence, they'd think twice about filling their homes with noisemakers.

I don't own a television set for that very reason; it
is a mindless annoyance that contributes little to
the well-being of one's soul. I feel the same way
about poodles.

Noise inhibits inward peace by distracting us
from spiritual self-examination. It keeps us from
discerning our soul's condition. Silence is the
spiritual knife which lays open our souls. If we
are never silent, we never have to examine the
truth about ourselves. This is why monks and
Quakers are quiet: so they can discover that
which can be found only in silence. But spiritual
self-examination is painful, which is why there
aren't a lot of monks and Quakers.

I was once talking with a Quaker woman
who had just lost her husband. "You'll think I'm
crazy," she told me, "but sometimes I talk out
loud and I pretend he is listening. Once I looked
over at his recliner and I could swear he was
there." She told how the Quaker silence didn't
bring her peace, but sorrow, because it
reminded her how alone she was. She and her
husband would sit in their recliners in the
evening and talk about the things husbands and
wives talk about—the children, the neighbors,
the president, and where to go on vacation. Now
there is no one to talk with, no voice to prop up

the other end of the conversation. I told her if she wanted to go to a church where they talked more, I would certainly understand.

Most of us need more silence than we get. Others of us have too much. The people who need silence don't get it. The ones who have silence often don't need it. This is a great problem in life, and if I only had enough silence, I could maybe figure out how to fix it.

CHAPTER TWENTY-FOUR

A Time to Speak

Yearly Meeting

Every August, we Quakers hold our annual business meeting in a sweltering barn of a room in Plainfield, Indiana. We've been doing that since 1856, so by now it's habit. On the second Thursday of August at high noon, we close up our homes and pilgrimage to Plainfield. You can set your watch by us.

My first visit was in 1977 for Sunday morning worship. I sat with Quakers from the Danville Meeting, right behind Lawson Barber. In addition to his kind heart, Lawson had an unusually long neck. I spent the hour counting how long it took a bead of sweat to make it from his hairline to shirt collar. I went home and told my father about Lawson Barber sweating and asked him why they didn't put in air-conditioning. He told me the Quakers didn't believe in air-conditioning and that's why there weren't a lot of them. Despite that, I decided to become a Quaker. In the dog days of summer, I regret that decision. But that's the only time. The rest of the time I enjoy being a Quaker, particularly in the fall and spring.

My parents air-conditioned their home a few years ago, the last ones in their neighborhood to do so except for Marvin and Lorena Rutledge, who are Quakers. Shortly thereafter, I stayed overnight at my parents' house. Slept upstairs in my old bed. It was just like when I was growing up, except for the air-conditioning. Back then we slept with the windows open, but it was still too hot to sleep. I'd lie in bed, listening to the train running on the tracks past Joe Johnson's farm. Every night at 11:07 that train would come through, heading west toward Illinois, Missouri, Kansas, and Colorado. When I was eighteen I wanted to be on that train. I wanted to be going far away. I didn't care where, just away.

Now with air-conditioning, the windows are closed and you can't hear the 11:07 when it passes. I listened, but couldn't hear it. I wonder what young people in that neighborhood dream about now that they can't hear the train.

My father doesn't like air-conditioning, so he sits out on the porch at night, drinking iced tea and smoking a cigarette. You can hear the swing creak back and forth and see the red glowing dot of his cigarette, watch it get brighter as he inhales. Before air-conditioning everyone used to pass the evening on their porches; now they stay inside and watch television. Except for my father, who sits out on that porch until the 11:07 passes. Then he finishes his cigarette, comes in, and goes to bed.

When we moved into that house thirty years ago, two big maple trees framed the front porch. After twenty-five years one of them died, the victim of carpenter ants and old age. Dad had it cut down. The yard looked lopsided. The other maple died that spring. Since death comes in threes, we held our breath and waited. Within a week, Lawson Barber passed. We counted the rings on the trees. Lawson and the trees were born the same year, an odd irony.

Those trees shaded the porch from the late-day

sun. Now the porch is a boiling cauldron. My
father has planted new trees, but it takes a long
time for trees to produce shade. He says the
porch won't be cool for another twenty years,
and by then he'll be gone. "Maybe you can enjoy
it," he tells me. "Maybe you can move back here
and live in this house and enjoy this porch the
way I have."

He had gotten a bid of six hundred dollars to
cut down the second tree, which at the time
seemed outrageous. Instead, he came across a
tree-trimming crew doing some work out by
Roy Manor's house on Old Highway 36 and they
offered to come by after work and cut down the
tree for three hundred dollars—cash. No questions asked. They said that twice: "No questions
asked."

That evening they came and cut off the
branches. Left twelve feet of trunk standing.
Came back the next evening to finish it off. They
started to cut into the base of that maple, but it
put up a fight and they ruined the blade of their
chain saw. They came back the next day with an
even bigger saw and they ruined that one, too.
Finally, on the fourth day, they brought that tree
down. In the center of the ancient tree was a
cement post which the tree had grown around

years before we moved there.

They left the tree trunk lying in Dad's yard. They haven't been back and Dad doesn't know how to get hold of them. Their phone number was one of the questions he couldn't ask. The tree is too heavy to move. That post is in it, so Dad can't cut it. It lies there on the ground, a twelve-foot tree trunk with a cement heart. That maple was such a beautiful tree. All those years we had marveled at its beauty, never dreaming it had a heart of stone. Its outward charm belied its inward hardness.

The Sunday morning I watched Lawson Barber sweat, the minister was teaching how our inward condition is more important than our outward appearance. "Take no thought for what ye shall wear," he said, paraphrasing Jesus. Even at the age of sixteen, it was obvious to me most of the folks in that room hadn't taken much thought about what they were wearing. These were not fashionable people; they leaned toward polyester and plaid. But instead of scorning their apparel, I valued their priorities.

We live in a skin-deep world. We spend more time in front of mirrors than we do in prayer. Pretty on the outside; hard at the core. Those of us who need most to go inward are fixated on the outward. Lawson Barber was nodding his head as the minister spoke. Taking it to heart. But Lawson didn't need to learn that lesson. The folks who needed to learn it weren't paying attention. Isn't that so often the case?

On the opening day of our annual meeting, we read aloud the names of the Quakers who died the year past. Victims of car crashes, cancers, old age, and, one sad year, a beloved pastor with Lou Gehrig's disease. If they don't read my name, I thank God for another year and take my seat. After the names are read, we comment on the deceased. Out of politeness, we find something good to say about each person, though the careful listener can discern that some persons are easier to praise than others.

The year Lawson died, we had plenty to say. Some told of his tireless work in the church. Others spoke of how he was gentle at the core. I wished he'd been there to hear it. No awkward pauses. No straining hard to remember something, anything, decent about this man. Just one voice after another telling of his goodness.

I still assemble with the Quakers the second week of August. Everything else in my life has changed except for this one immovable, immutable fact: August will find me in a sweltering barn of a room in Plainfield. Not much there has changed, except that Lawson is gone and others with him, their names a quiet reverberation in a barn of a room.

I hope when my name is read, there'll be no awkward pauses. I hope they can say my heart was good, my core tender. When I was eighteen and listening to the trains and dreaming, that wasn't the dream I had for myself. Now it seems as fine a hope as any, and better than most.

CHAPTER TWENTY-FIVE

A Time to Love

Loving Our Neighbor

Some of my deepest blessings in life came by accident.

My mother met my father while playing in a football game at the age of eleven. She almost went to the movies that day but decided to play football instead. If she had gone to the movies, I wouldn't be here.

If a friend of mine hadn't told me about a certain vacant apartment, then I would have moved somewhere else and wouldn't have met my wife.

If Paul Harvey Jr. and Dina Kinnan hadn't fallen in love, I might never have had a book published.

Some people get where they are through hard work and savvy. I rely on dumb luck and accidents of fate. Somewhere in the back of my head is the idea that God might occasionally stack the deck in my favor. There is too much blessing, too much coincidence for luck and fate to be the only factors at work in my life.

"Coincidence," says Madeleine L' Engle, "is God working anonymously."

The best luck I've had lately is moving next door to Libby Eddy. When we first looked at our house, the realtor gave us a computer printout detailing its virtues. It listed three fireplaces, a dining room, a living room, a basement, three and a half baths, four bedrooms, a two-car garage, and a cool breezeway for summer naps. But not one word about Libby Eddy. At the bottom of the page, where they name the extras, it read *Stove, dishwasher, and window treatments stay.* But no sentence saying, *Kind woman next door will love your family and dispense sound advice, but only when asked.* The best things about a house seldom get mentioned on the computer printout the realtor gives you.

This is a new neighborhood of young families finding their way. Libby and her husband built their house in October 1955; thirty-five years later a developer built a horseshoe of houses around Libby. She is our center, our anchor, our resident sage. In every neighborhood I have lived, there has been one wise person whose life radiates good sense and solid virtue. We young people move in, flush with pride and full of ourselves, snickering at these old-fashioned people, but within a year we are knocking on their doors asking advice.

*B*ack when people didn't move far from home, they turned to their parents and grandparents for counsel. Today, with families sprawled across the nation, there is no one to talk to and we make terrible decisions. How can we ask Grandma's advice over a plate of cookies if Grandma's a thousand miles away in her Florida condo? All that wisdom gone to waste. I blame every social ill on this sad fact of modern life.

Libby Eddy is a retired horticulturist. We wander over to her house to ask what kind of trees we should plant and end up asking her counsel on matters of child rearing, investing, and who to hire to paint our house. She is a big believer in hard maples and blue spruces, in rearing children with clear expectations and much affection, in blue-chip stocks, and in Larry Hart, the painter.

There is a man in our town who, ten years ago, sold his house and journeyed to California to meet a New Age guru and unlock the mysteries of the universe. He came back three months later, flat broke and none the wiser. Libby would have talked to him for free.

I've known Libby Eddy since I was in the first grade and her son, Bill, invited me home to play after school. She was waiting for us with homemade cookies and iced tea, a service she often provides. I called her Mrs. Eddy then and when I first moved back, but after a few weeks she told me to call her Libby, so I do. My boys call her Miss Libby. I've told them they'd better-by-golly mind their manners around her.

We've been holding our breath around here. In the past five years, Libby has been hit with two cancers. She won the first round, and when we recently moved in next to her she was dazed and reeling from her second go-round. I almost didn't befriend her for fear her death was near and the loss would be too painful. But it's impossible to live next door to Libby and not be her friend. Within a week she had me at her kitchen table eating cookies and drinking iced tea. She brewed it, squinted at me (she looks a bit like Katharine Hepburn), and asked, "Do you still drink your tea sweetened?"

I write upstairs in my house, in the bedroom under the eaves. The window looks out on Libby's house. We moved here in midspring. I would watch Libby from the window as she tottered on her cane around her yard, weak from cancer and a broken bone. Her children, Bill and Kathy, made her promise she wouldn't work, but as soon as their truck cleared the driveway she'd climb on her mower and steer back and forth across the yard. Her one concession to the illness was allowing Larry and Merrily Nilles to carry the morning paper to her doorstep.

Bill visited her at lunchtime. I work with my window open and could hear his truck coming down the road and turning in. He would climb from his truck, walk up the sidewalk, open her front door, and ask in a loud voice, "How are we feeling today?" He is a faithful son. When the cancer was at its worst, he was there most every day. Kathy phoned her in the evenings after work and came to visit on weekends. If I ever get cancer and my kids fuss over me like Libby's children have, I'll be grateful.

By autumn, Libby was walking without her cane and was spreading mulch on her rose bushes. She walked over to visit one October afternoon. I was mowing, and Joan was playing ball with the boys in the side yard. I shut off the mower and walked over to where Libby was standing with my wife.

"I've just come from my doctor," she told us. "He says the cancer is gone. I've made it. I've survived."

We hugged her and beamed. Wonderful, glorious victory. The boys smiled. They didn't quite understand the news but suspected it was good. I climbed back on my mower and glanced back at Libby and Joan, who were talking and laughing. Joan is very fond of Libby. Her mother lives two hours away and Libby is right across the street. Joan will bake an extra portion of food and carry it over to Libby's, an excuse to sit in her living room and visit.

Joan comes home and tells me, "I hope when I'm Libby's age, I'm just like her." I hope I'm around to see that. Libby's husband isn't. He died in 1993. I think of all the grief Libby has shouldered in five years' time and marvel at her strength. But then strength doesn't come through ease and comfort and smooth sailing.

I'm planning to landscape my backyard. Libby told me about farmers down the road who stack fieldstone at the corners of their fields, free for the taking. She told me the best place to buy topsoil and shrubs and trees and when to plant them.

"Try a black maple tree," she said. "They're a wonderful tree."

I went to the nursery and asked a young man, fresh from college, if they had any black maple trees. He laughed and said there was no such tree. An old man in bib overalls, a nursery worker standing nearby, interrupted. "Oh, yes, there is. They're a wonderful tree, but no one asks for them anymore. Where'd you learn about black maple trees?"

I drew myself up and said that anyone who knows anything about trees knows about black maple trees. I looked at the young man as I spoke, the young whippersnapper.

I intend to spend quite a few winter after-noons at Libby's house planning out my landscaping. She has pictures and books and various other horticultural materials to show me. We've cleared our calendars and are going to work.

I could have lived anywhere in the world. I had the good fortune to move next door to Libby Eddy. When I lie in bed at night, the light outside her barn spills through our window and bathes the room, light amidst the darkness.

Jesus commands us to love our neighbors. Such an easy thing for me to do.

CHAPTER TWENTY-SIX

A Time to Hate

When We Were Children

When I was a teenager and became a Quaker, the pastor called to tell me someone from the church would be appointed to teach me the faith.

I was hoping they would send an alluring teenage girl to be my mentor, a beauty who would sit on the couch beside me and, over the course of many evenings, instruct me in the Christian life. Instead, they sent Carolyn Kellum, who was in her late sixties and a pacifist—the first pacifist I had ever met. Such a novelty! She almost made me forget about teenage girls. Almost.

Everyone else I knew said things like, "Of course I don't like war, but…" then would name the circumstances in which a Christian might hate someone enough to shoot him dead. Carolyn told me point blank that Christians were commanded to love, not hate, their enemies. Case closed.

"Don't you believe those preachers who tell you it is possible to love your enemy and still kill them. It can't be done," she said.

That was twenty years ago, and ever since then I've been trying to find a way to hate certain people and still walk close to Jesus, but without success. If you've found a way to do that, let me know. There are several people I would love to hate if I thought I could get away with it.

As long as I can remember I've been trying to figure out what it means to be grown-up. My older son is six years old. When I was his age, I thought being grown-up came with age. Of course, that isn't true. We all know people who are in their fifties and haven't grown up.

When my Grandma Norma was a little girl, she thought a grown-up was someone who could eat ice cream whenever he or she wanted.

When I was a teenager, I thought a grown-up was someone who had sex. I suspect a lot of teenagers think that, which is why so many of them experiment with sex. It took me several years, and much pain, to learn that real grown-ups don't allow their hormones to make those decisions best left to the brain.

When I graduated from high school, I thought grown-ups were people who got jobs and supported themselves. I was partially right. Of course, being grown-up means much more than taking care of yourself, but it's a good start. There are some people who never get that far.

When I married my wife and we started a family, I thought a grown-up was someone who took good care of not only himself but also his family. Someone who could lay aside personal gratification for the good of another. Someone who chose staying home over bar-hopping, who went to the P.T.A. meeting instead of staying home to watch the game. That is a big part of what it means to be grown-up—the ability to care for others as well as self, to lay aside personal desires for the good of someone you love. But that is not all.

There is more.

$\mathcal{U}$ltimately, to be grown-up means that wisdom, reason, and love dictate our choices, as opposed to emotions, lusts, and urges.

For example, people who commit adultery or who sacrifice their families on the altar of their careers have surrendered to emotions, lusts, and urges. They have failed to make important decisions based on wisdom, reason, and love. They live as children, not as adults.

If we allow ourselves to hate other persons and make choices on the basis of hate, rather than on the basis of wisdom, reason, and love, we are not grown-up. For we are allowing our emotions and urges to dictate our actions. Grown-ups don't do that; children do.

A big problem in our world today is that many grown-ups haven't grown up. Their life choices are driven by emotion, lusts, and urges, unchecked by any sense of morality, reason, or wisdom. They lust without reserve. They satisfy every material longing. They neglect those who count on them. They give hate free reign in their lives. Consequently, they have not grown up. They walk around in adult bodies. They are entrusted with adult responsibilities. But they ultimately bring ruination to themselves and others because their life choices are driven by the wrong forces.

Now I want to tell you a lie. Hate is an emotion we can't help. Hate is a feeling we cannot overcome. If we hate someone, it is because we just can't help ourselves. We're human. We have no choice but to hate. That is a lie. Unfortunately, it is a lie many people believe. They believe this lie in order to excuse their hatred. After all, if we can't help but hate, if hate is a feeling we simply cannot help, then hatred is never our fault, is it?

But we *can* help it. Hatred is a choice. We choose to hate, just as we choose to love. Oh, I know, there are people out there who believe love isn't a choice, that love is primarily an emotion, a feeling, a stirring in the loins. These are the same people who stay married for six months, then divorce. These are the people who love the idea of love but seem unable to stay in it. Love is a matter of the will—something we decide to do. Love is a choice.

And so is hatred. Hatred is something we decide to do. We can hate our ex-spouse, but we don't have to. It is our choice. We can hate Muslims, but we don't have to. It is our choice. We can hate black people or white people or yellow people, but we don't have to. It is our choice. We can hate homosexuals, but we don't have to. It is our choice. Hatred, like love, is a choice.

Hatred is the refuge of those who won't grow up. Haters are moral infants, perennial children, tantrum throwers who haven't gotten their way. When my six-year-old is that way, I can understand it. I don't excuse it, but I understand. Then I work hard to make sure he doesn't stay that way. I let him know in no uncertain terms that hatred is not acceptable. It is scary to think how many people turn their children loose in the world without ever teaching them that.

*I*f there is a time to hate, as Ecclesiastes suggests, it is when we are children, when we don't know any better, when we think hate is something we can't help. The apostle Paul knew this. In 1 Corinthians 13, he observed that when he was a child, he spoke, thought, and reasoned as a child. But when he grew up, he put aside childish ways. Since Paul was writing about love, I think the childish thing he laid aside was hate. When Paul laid aside hate, when Paul grew up, he was able to appreciate the transforming power of love.

This is what Carolyn Kellum was trying to
teach me when I first became a Christian. But I
was too busy thinking about teenage girls to pay
her any mind. This was back in the days when I
spoke, thought, and reasoned as a child. Now
I'm trying to set aside my childish ways. It isn't
easy. Spiritual maturity is a lifelong process,
accomplished one choice at a time.

Sometimes, after reading newspaper accounts
of killings far and near, I lay aside the paper,
close my eyes, and dream of a world where the
only thing people hate is hatred.

CHAPTER TWENTY-SEVEN

A Time for War

Civil Defense

After six months of living back in this town, I realized the black-and-yellow civil defense signs were gone.

They used to flank each entrance of the courthouse. There were also signs outside Hargrave Hall at the Central Normal Teachers College and in the basement of the Christian Church on Main Street. In the event of a nuclear war, we were to proceed with our families to the courthouse, the college, or the Christian Church, where we would wait out the war and emerge unscathed to resume our lives.

If we were at school when the Bomb hit, we were to do the same as we did during tornado drills—sit in the hallway with our heads between our legs. Three times a year, we practiced this routine. Mr. Michaels would announce on the intercom that a bomb was on the way. We would rise solemnly to our feet, march to the hallway, and assume our positions. I would sit with my head between my legs, worrying about my parents and whether they had made it to the courthouse in time. After a while, I learned to tell the difference between a drill and the real thing. If after telling us a bomb was on the way, Mr. Michaels then read the lunch menu, I knew it was only a drill.

We lived near the courthouse, so that was where our family was supposed to go if the siren sounded three times. One blast on the siren meant it was lunchtime. Wally Clark would lay down his wrench at Logan's Mobil and head for lunch at the Coffee Cup Cafe. Two blasts meant a tornado. We would run to our basements. Three blasts meant a bomb was on the way. A couple times a year it blasted twice. Whenever it did, we would listen anxiously for a third blast, which never came. We would hurry to our basements, thanking God it was only a tornado.

As a child, I worried that the Russians might have poor aim—that instead of bombing the

Allison Engine Company twenty miles to our east, they might miss and hit our town instead. The Russians, I had been taught, were godless Communists who would force us to disown our Christian faith or die. As a child, I had a strong sense of drama and imagined the entire town renouncing their faith, while I alone held fast. But the Russians never came, to the strong disappointment of the men in our town who had spent countless hours planning our defense and those of us who dreamed of a martyr's death.

*C*olonel C. Kerney worked in our town's civil defense program. He was a veteran of World War II and a member of Mary, Queen of Peace Catholic Church, where his wife, Dorothy, played the organ for twenty-seven years. He drove an army green van and wore army green pants tucked inside his army boots. He had three sons—Robert Lee Kerney, George Patton Kerney, and John Pershing Kerney. Plus two daughters, Margaret and Ann. Margaret was named for a saint and Ann was named Ann because every Ann that Mrs. Kerney knew was sweet, so that's what she named her daughter.

Colonel C. Kerney was a member of the

cavalry and fought in the last horse battle of
World War II. He fought in the Philippines
under General Douglas MacArthur, for whom
he did not name one of his sons. When the tide
turned against us in the Philippines, MacArthur
left but Colonel C. Kerney stayed put. The sup-
ply lines were cut off and the cavalry troops had
to eat their horses to keep from starving. The
men were captured by the Japanese and impris-
oned. Colonel C. Kerney was the first officer to
escape the prisoner-of-war camp and return to
the fighting. When Douglas MacArthur left the
Philippines he vowed to return, but Colonel C.
Kerney of Danville, Indiana, got there first.

When I was young and sitting in our pew at
Mary, Queen of Peace Catholic Church, I would
watch Colonel Kerney and his family, three pews
up. I would wonder about him. There was no
one else like him in our whole town, and I didn't
know what to make of him. This was during the
Vietnam War, when militarism was suspect;
being young, I dismissed the colonel as a relic
and had nothing to do with him.

In all the years I lived here my thoughts
about him never changed. When I moved away,
I forgot about him. Then I came home and
noticed the civil defense signs were gone and he

with them. He had died in 1991. With Colonel Kerney gone, when the signs fell down there was no one to replace them.

*I*t wasn't until I talked with his widow that I learned these things about Colonel Kerney. I never knew he fought in World War II. Never knew he almost starved to death. Never knew he was a prisoner of war. Never knew he escaped and went back to the fighting. I wished I had known. Maybe I would have had kinder thoughts about him. I'm not sure. I was young and lacking in appreciation.

Two of the most dedicated pacifists I know are friends of mine—George Rubin and Ray Stewart. Both became Quaker pacifists after fighting in World War II. This is a mystery to me—how fighting in a war can cause some people to become pacifists and cause others to name their sons for generals. I know that after the war, George and Ray and Colonel Kerney did what each thought right. I wouldn't dare condemn their choices for fear of dishonoring their contributions, which I do appreciate.

My older son attends the same school I did. Three times a year they have a tornado drill. The children march solemnly into the hallway where they sit with their heads between their legs. They no longer have bomb drills. There is no need. I am not certain who to thank for that— Ray and George or Colonel C. Kerney. But I am grateful that my son doesn't have the worries I had. And I pray to God that never changes.

CHAPTER TWENTY-EIGHT

A Time for Peace

Summer

The full splendor of our town is not fully revealed until summer. In winter we are like any other small town. The snow turns gray after a week, the sun doesn't shine, and we bust our tires on chuckholes. Autumn is better than winter, but there are leaves to rake. Besides, winter is on its way and that dampens our enthusiasm. Fall is like living under the shadow of a terminal illness. Spring is exquisite, except for the tornadoes, which make it difficult to relax. This makes summer the perfect season—no chuckholes, no leaves to rake, and no tornadoes. A time for peace.

In the summer, our scramble slows to an

amble. The schools close and the churches move to summer hours. Up in the city they are dabbling in year-round school. This is heresy of the highest order and would never fly in these parts. Certain educators claim that giving children the summer off means they won't be learning three months of the year, which is not only false but arrogant. Children need to learn many lessons, only some of which are taught in schools.

So far during summers, I have taught my sons how to catch a baseball, how to pick off ticks, how to find the Big Dipper, how to make hummingbird food, and the best way to paint a porch swing. When our electricity went out, I taught them how to power up a generator and trim a lamp wick. They can tell a male cardinal from a female and they know not to eat chokeberries.

While I have made progress with my boys, there is still much they need to learn.

I need to teach my boys how to sharpen a lawn mower blade and change the oil in the mower. They need to learn how to patch bicycle tires and bait a fishhook and clean their catch. They don't know how to tell if sweet corn is ready to pick or even how to cook it. They can't ride without training wheels. I haven't shown them how to clothespin a baseball card to the front fork of a bicycle so it flicks against the spokes and makes an engine-noise, how to build a fort from a refrigerator box, or how to grow gourds for birdhouses. These are all good things to know that schools can't teach them. That's why God created summer.

When I pastored in the city, I was amazed to learn they held Sunday school during the summer months. I put an end to it by showing them in the Bible how Sunday school was supposed to end on Memorial Day and resume on Labor Day. It's right there in the Old Testament, up near the front amidst all the rules.

"It's a matter of holy obedience," I told them, so for the eight years I pastored there, that's what we did. I also canceled most of the committee meetings held during the summer. Summer is not the time to be sitting in a church basement conducting business. If you have to meet, you drop by the house after supper and talk on the porch.

I also didn't like to counsel people during the summer. When people called with problems, I advised them to take a walk around the block and visit with their neighbors. There are few afflictions that can't be made better by a summer evening stroll. I have seen depressions lifted, marriages healed, and drunkards reformed by summer rambles. If walks don't help, a frosty mug of root beer from the Mug-N-Bun will cure the most dogged ailment. A wondrous elixir, root beer. On more than one occasion I've driven a quivering, weakened soul to the Mug-N-Bun, held a mug of root beer to their feeble lips, and watched them spring to life. The Mug-N-Bun is only open in the summer, another reason for that season's unrivaled glory.

These are just a few of our town's summertime splendors; there are others, chief among them the children's park program. The park program was begun in 1948 and has been going ever since. They hired Mr. Robert Leedy to oversee the softball games, which he did every summer for thirty years. Rosemary Helton taught tennis and the women of Tri Kappa taught the smaller children crafts like how to make pictures from macaroni and pencil holders from soup cans.

I was six years old when I started in the park program and stuck with it through high school.

Two hours of softball every morning, Monday through Friday, under the watchful gaze of Robert Leedy. We called it Leedyball. Mr. Leedy was thin as a straw, had a kind word for everyone and a remarkable talent for telling time by the sun.

"What time is it, Mr. Leedy?" we would ask him.

He would peer at the sun, his hands shading his eyes. "Nine forty-eight," he'd reply. None of us had watches to verify his accuracy, but he answered with such conviction that we never doubted him.

Mr. Leedy died in 1989, but not before grooming his successor, Steve Johnson, who heads up the park program today. Steve has been at it since 1974. In that time he has instituted a few changes. They used to hold Popsicle Day every Thursday, but the Popsicle money has gotten thin, so now it's done only once a month. On the plus side, he has Milton Stout bring his miniature horses for the kids to pet. And the Indianapolis Indians, Indiana's Triple-A minor league baseball team, sends a player to extol the winsome beauty of baseball.

Once a summer the fire department comes with its truck and takes the kids for a loop around the park.

Monday through Friday, nine-thirty in the morning, I drive my boys to the park program. Two hours later I pick them up. They are young yet, so they work on crafts. They come home with pictures made from macaroni and pencil holders made from soup cans.

A couple days a week they play softball. They come home and discuss it over lunch, telling of pop flies, grounders, and other wonders.

"Mr. Johnson can tell time by the sun," they report.

I marvel aloud at that rare skill.

In the fifty-plus years of the program, they've never raised the prices. It started out free and still is. I asked Steve Johnson where the money comes from.

"I have no idea," he told me.

My father used to serve on the town board. I asked him where the money came from. Taxes, he said. Except for the Popsicle money, which now comes from the Tri Kappa ladies. This is a Republican town, a populace averse to taxes of every stripe. But any suggestion to scale back the park program and save a little money raises howls. It's bad enough we had to cut back on the Popsicles, people say.

I live in this town because in 1957 my father took a job in Indianapolis and my parents drove through here on their way to the city to look for a house. They came through on a Saturday morning in the summer. But instead of barreling past on Highway 36, Dad hung a right at the five-and-dime and looped around the square. It was the very morning Johnston's Regal Grocery had hired a cowboy to do rope tricks on the sidewalk in front of their store, right next to a sign that read *Come Lasso A Deal! Ground Beef—Three Pounds for a Dollar!*

My sister saw that cowboy from the backseat of their Plymouth Belvedere and yelled to be let out of the car. Dad pulled over to the curb and they climbed out for a closer look. They stood there watching that cowboy, in his boots and high hat, twirling his rope on a Saturday morning in the summer.

There was another man present, thin as a straw, a Mr. Robert Leedy, who talked with my parents about the park program and Popsicle

Day and how to tell time by the sun. By the time they climbed back in their car, Mom and Dad had resolved to settle here.

When I was eighteen, I left town. For good, I thought. Twenty years later I am back. Mr. Robert Leedy is gone, but Steve Johnson is here and there's talk of resurrecting Popsicle Day. Steve Johnson promises to someday teach me how to tell time by the sun, which is one more thing you won't learn in school and why summer is the finest season of all.

There was a time I was grateful to God only for my obvious blessings. Now what I treasure are these subtle glories—the steady peace of a summer morning and two small boys with so much yet to learn.